THE INSUFFICIENCY OF REPARATIONS

The Evolved Thoughts Of One Older White Man

GARY ADORNATO

Copyright © Gary Adornato, Washington, D.C. 2020

All rights reserved. No part of this publication may be reproduced, stored or transmitted in any form or by any means, electronic, mechanical, photocopying, recording, scanning, or otherwise without written permission from the publisher. It is illegal to copy this book, post it to a website, or distribute it by any other means without permission.

DEDICATION

To my parents Arthur and Lynn, whose own lives of openness and generosity taught me to expect that in the world, and to be indignant at its absence.

To my wife, partner (and editor) Fran, whose infinite love and support makes everything possible and everything better, and whose passion for social justice inspired this work.

To my children Brian and Pamela, and their spouses Shelly and Patrick, who have taught me far more by the example of their exceptional lives than I could have ever imagined, or have learned without them.

TABLE OF CONTENTS

FORWARD

What This Is, and What This Is Not

This is not intended as a scholarly dissertation. I lack the credentials and ability for such an undertaking, as well as the belief that I have the ability to produce it. I have chosen to avoid specifics in terms of the past transgressions in order not to distract from the analysis, relying on the irrefutable fact of generational abuse and racism.

Any reader who doubts the absolute truth of that historical and present condition is invited to read no further.

This is not a historical documentation of the nature and specifics of racial inequality. Most treatments of the subject of reparations offer a compendium of mistreatments, atrocities and broken promises, and are often particularly well done. This is not an attempt to add to that valuable body of work.

This is not intended as a definitive prescription. It is an offered perspective of one white man, somewhat older and long ago isolated from academia. It has a specific amount of detail because it is within those details that these suggestions can be best understood. It is not intended to be the sole basis for legislation or policy.

This book is a presentation of ideas intended to create conversation and further analysis. Any actual application would require a massive effort by multiple groups over an extended period of time, as well as decisions on allocating costs, selecting funding mechanisms, incorporation into existing and new legislative programs, etc. That said, by including references to specific outcomes and applications, it is hoped that some or all of these proposals will inspire others to consider undertaking that hard work.

I pray that I, and this work, will come to represent a single voice in a massive choir, rather than a solo of any particular note.

This is a particularly time-sensitive document. It is my hope that it represents a specifically transitional work, one whose contribution and relevancy is only pertinent to the time and conditions of its publication. In a perfect world, it might serve as a historical reference to a time before awareness and action, something to be marveled at with a shaken head, as in "...was that really necessary to be said back then?..." In a sadly more likely outcome, it might become useful again as history repeats.

In simplifying an immensely complicated issue, it will likely appear that I've ignored the nuances behind those complications. As I explain more fully later in this book, I am not suggesting that the trauma of enslavement is unworthy of restitution, nor am I arguing against those champions of reparations who call for answers to promises broken and acres unprovided. My approach here is to ponder only the ponderable, to address what might be, in some limited way, quantifiable. I cannot adequately consider the placing of a financial compensation for the horrors inflicted on human beings placed into bondage.

I have a dear friend who lost his youthful son in an accident; he once asked me to put myself in his shoes, and I lovingly refused. There is an anguish there that I cannot share without presuming the same tragedy to my own beloved children, and I cannot go there and come back again whole.

I accept my inability and cowardice, and simply do not question or equate the pain held by anyone else; it is an impossible ask. I grieve instead for my friend in the present, for the ache of his memory rather than the experience of his loss. It is such for me with slavery, and the malevolent realities of that national sin. I can grieve for and try to comprehend the resultant impact and existing unfairness, but to contemplate the incomprehensible inhumanity of the actual experience… again, I cannot go there, and come back whole.

I have a far more pragmatic reason for not dealing directly with slavery as the sole origination of reparational compensation; I find it far too narrow, far too excluding to use as the boundary line. The systemic implementation of inequality in America did not end with the freeing of the slaves, and the inflicted penalties were not exclusive to those who came directly from their line. Our national racism has asked no question other than the color of skin in choosing whom to deprive. The family arriving from the Caribbean in the 1920's were no less prevailed upon than the descendants of a slave;

European Blacks had no privileges beyond those whose recent ancestors were African.

Reparations should not seek to calibrate the losses according to generational presence or geographic origination; those were not the terms of the discrimination. It was, and far too often still is, simply racism.

Too often, the proponents of reparations — even the most articulate — attempt to soften the economic blow by announcing that they are not seeking compensation from people, but rather from the federal government. This is suggested as if funds that were derived from the government were somehow magically created. As an economist, I see this as a deceit, beneath the level of seriousness that the topic deeply deserves. The U.S. government has no money of its own, but is rather the steward of the people's money that it has collected in the form of taxes. The financing of any restitution will be, as it most certainly should be, a product of allocating the people's money for that purpose. We must own up to that, and not hide behind misdirections or gentle words.

This book is a personal expression of my own evolved thoughts, perspectives and opinions. Those are the product of just one life, a life that has never spent a day inside of a Black skin, and that has never held a Black child in his arms and tried to explain the unexplainable. While I have done my best to understand, I neither suggest that I have that insight, nor do I accept the argument that its absence precludes the relevancy of my opinions on this crucial topic.

I am acutely aware that, in a disappointingly large number of published circles, my contributions to this subject are unwelcome. As a white male, I have read that I am a trespasser who should support, but not seek to direct or overtly influence the conversations, let alone propose solutions. I have recently read that the increasing volume of white participants in the Black Lives Matter movement is a form of cultural appropriation.

I find such suggestions equally offensive and short-sighted. The offensive part is that some still believe this to be only a "Black" issue and not a deeply American concern and critical humanitarian value. It is a bias that needs to be rooted out and eliminated in order for any important outcomes to emerge. The short-sighted part is the lack of an understanding that any conversation that is not inclusive, that does not hear and understand the perspectives of all of the stakeholders with equal clarity and enthusiasm, is ultimately futile.

I do not want to simply ignore those criticisms. I want to actively argue against them, and to reject the limitations that they seek to put on the contributions to and ultimate success of a process critical to the health and recovery of our shared nation. I have no intention of censoring or diluting my beliefs, whether here or elsewhere.

Real movement towards reparations can only emerge through mutual acceptance of its appropriateness, not through the application of force or the perception of extortion. I can not envision any scenario where an unconvinced America submits to protest or forced coercion as the basis for accepting programs and policies on a relevant, transformative scale.

Through protracted demonstration and media support there has been some token response achieved, but any acceptance of such minor concessions as a form of resolution would be painfully counter-productive. It would allow white America to consider the matter settled and fully paid for without having made the hard changes that are required, without having made the necessary commitments, and without having laid a solid foundation for future racial balance.

The definition and implementation of a sufficient response to systemic racism must evolve from a national agreement. I believe that to achieve enough of a consensus, it will require a demonstrated and broadly accepted logic, an undeniable correlation between the damage done and the offered repair, and a defined and executable path towards balance and reconciliation.

This document is my contribution to that process.

CHAPTER ONE

A Personal Journey

What entitles anyone to dare suggest a solution to a problem as complicated, as full of emotion and personal resonance, as the issue of racial inequality and injustice?

I contend that it is precisely the enormity of the challenge that demands that each of us provide what we can, derived from what we know and seasoned by what we believe.

The transformative quilt that must ultimately emerge will not come from a single bolt of fabric, but from the assembled patches of every cloth and dye contributed by thousands of unique perspectives. It is when the diversity of input matches the complexity of the challenge that we can begin to choose the pieces that fit, the pattern of the whole.

I build things in the financial and business worlds. My patch of the quilt then will come from that skillset, those experiences. In prescribing these actions, I offer what I have and what I am, in the hopes that it will either produce a useful square, or inspire someone else to share a better one.

I believe that most of us have core elements of self-identification, qualities that we hold particularly close and proudly so. These are the ones that we tell ourselves are our personal super powers, those aspects that we bring out when we want to do good in the world, to demonstrate our own value to ourselves, to others, or to God.

I have understood my own powers since early childhood. I have a good and reasonably demonstrated ability to solve problems, that I use to bring to bear a number of intellectual tools and to coalesce available resources. This skill has allowed me to travel a fairly unique road in my professional life, to experience a seemingly unrelated group of industries and partnerships constructively and without restraint.

That confidence in my capacity to create a positive outcome has led me to venture without hesitation in whatever direction my curiosity leads me, and my curiosity is fairly insatiable. In believing that I can help to resolve situations where and when I find them, there has been no reason to stay in some kind of lane, and I have not.

For these purposes, I'll refer to my other power as empathy. For better or worse (and often for both) I cannot avoid strong feelings for those close to me, to feel committed to their challenges and to their support. As I believe that I am called to do, I begin each new relationship with love and allow it to move as it will from that lofty position. In the world of business in America that is not always a positive or useful quality, but it has yielded a lifetime of friends and experiences that make any negatives irrelevant.

It is magnified infinitely in my most fortunate and admittedly rare of foundations, an uninterrupted outpouring of family love and support, from my parents and my siblings, from my wife and our children, through their loved ones and the gift of my grandson, and from a long list of extraordinary friends. I am, in this area (and therefore in all ways) undeservedly blessed and strengthened. As my son once shared, if whenever I come home I am so unconditionally loved, what is there to fear in the world?

I consider this second quality to be the unquestioned driver of the first. If I have the capacity to contribute to making the life of someone that I love better, what a privilege to use that skill on that behalf. And if I love those that I encounter, then I am called to do what I can to the best of my ability, wherever I find an opportunity.

This is how I find myself here, in this time and place. For months, the anguish and fear all around me has been palpable, overwhelming. My wife and I have held each other close, feeling too powerless against the vitriol and conflict. Absent a better response, I went to my computer and began writing, trying to use social media for the first time to insert myself into the middle of that battlefield, hoping to find something that I could help heal, help make sense of and for.

That immersion has led me to a conclusion: that the current federal politics and policies, arguments and negotiations are too superficial to be truly meaningful. As this is being written, the arms of government are constantly floating trial balloons in an effort to see how little or how much they can get away with. The present administration is uninterested in the issues of race and justice, and likely won't be a willing partner in any important solutions. Any serious and substantial legislation won't occur until after the 2020 election dust clears, and by then there will be major competition for early space on the various agendas regardless of the winning side.

Of equal importance, the current protests and movements -- while irreplaceably vital to getting and keeping the attention of the country -- are too fragmented and localized to create real pressure nationally for a major reinvention. The growing power of the moment must ultimately come together around a series of concrete positions and demands. It must focus its influence on a sharply defined and clearly articulated set of priorities in order to elevate any idea of reparations into the national discussion.

In the matter of racial inequality, resolution cannot be relevant so long as it rests on a rotted foundation, a tilted playing field that mocks any attempts at balance on top of it. It is that revelation that led me to explore the potential metrics of systemic change, and to embrace that most-charged word: Reparation. It was in that difficult idea that I found an approach that made philosophical and economic sense to me.

It was with that word in mind that I determined to work towards identifying and contributing towards a potential outcome, one that I could endorse as pertinent and constructive, one that might offer a vision of a somewhat better future America than the present one.

The methodology that I chose to apply is largely the same through which I approach challenges in business and in life: a consideration of a best case objective, an understanding of the available resources and capacities and their application, and a defined and executable path to resolution. Just as in much of the business universe, I can neither compel adoption nor implement the result; I can simply suggest what I see, and offer it for consideration.

CHAPTER TWO

Contradictions, Definitions and Calculations

When we seek to put action to words, we must focus on the intention and objectives of their definitions. Reparations is one example where the extreme importance of the outcome demands clarity in analysis, and a rejection of superficiality.

In the current usage, reparations have evolved into a simplistic function: the paying of money to the descendants of slaves as compensation for their unpaid labors. I contend that this is a gross misrepresentation. What was denied of Black men and women – by governing law, by force and by society – was not a fair wage, but their very humanity based solely on their race.

When we identify that as the true transgression, then the appropriate compensation is clearly not a check, but is a restoration of what was taken. That taking was not limited to just one era in American history, but has persisted through all the generations of Black Americans that have come since, regardless of their place of origin or the timing of their arrival.

Accepting that truth, reparations must be redefined as a dynamic, comprehensive effort toward balancing the privileges, status and resources that Black citizens have in the current world with what they rightfully should have in an equitable system. Therefore, the definition of reparations must be adapted to include the continuing impact of the original racism on an entire portion of Americans, and the present inequities.

The concept of reparations is almost as old as slavery in America. From the beginning, the practice of human bondage has caused some who engaged in it to challenge themselves, their faith and their actions loudly even as they bid on the next Black family from a ship's dark hold. Famously, Thomas Jefferson wrote volumes on the subject. He professed slavery to be "a moral depravity" and anticipated the abject punishment of a displeased God. He called for the abolishment of slavery in multiple texts, both in the governance of Virginia and in the founding of the new Republic.

He also owned over 600 people, spawned a second family with his slave Sally Hemmings, and still declined to call for their freedom upon his own death, as was a common practice among others with similar internal conflicts.

There is no reconciling the choices that were made, no excusing the Faustian bargain accepted in seeking financial prosperity through the enslavement of others. There is nothing to say except that it was amoral and for America, the original sin that gained the new country material advantages at the cost of its emerging soul.

For every generation since that time, there have been innumerable fatalities of the most horrific kind in the cause of racism, an uninterrupted line that only paused for a second to pass through the callously ended life of George Floyd under the knee of a police officer. Those transgressions have grown as a festering wound on the heart of America as they have been graphically exposed by technology, precluding plausible denial and finally forcing open a poison ledger.

Beyond the taking of a life is the continuous and continuing theft of the rights, the freedoms, the opportunities and the dreams of an entire people for generation after generation. Over one eighth of Americans are Black, and the systemic disadvantages imposed on all of their lives have been unrelenting, imposing an incalculable cost on many tens of millions of citizens across centuries, and into the present.

There is a twisted illogic to the perpetuation of gross injustice to the present day, a mathematical equation that joins the inarguable moral one in not only demanding change, but making the resistance to it inconceivable. There has never been a profit to be made turning down a paying customer at a diner seat, never a benefit gained in not hiring the person most able to do a job. In actively denying equality in development and engagement, America has deprived itself of the inestimable contributions of fully one eighth of its citizens, and critically handicapped its progress and success.

Racial injustice is a heinous crime that also steals from the criminal, rather than enriching him. It has always been, and remains, a blight that divides and weakens our nation, both domestically and in the eyes of a world that we seek to lead. Resistance to its eradication is not only morally unjustifiable, but demonstrably unprofitable.

It is only the methodology of the eradication of racial injustice, not the appropriateness or urgency, that is worth discussing and debating.

There is a convenience to the conventional idea of reparations, a simplicity that makes it almost palatable for so many on both sides of the Black and white divide. For the Black American, it may be a minimalist recognition by their oppressors of the most graphic of their victimization, some grudging acknowledgement of a history that has been almost too painful to contemplate for centuries. For the white American, it could be a type of "indulgence", a financial payment for the forgiveness of sins as was fashionable in the Christian church during Medieval times. It is a balm to a guilty conscious that frees white America from the expansive costs of true repentance and reform.

Reparations is defined in most dictionaries as financial compensation to the descendants of slaves for their enslavement. It is simple, clean, tangible. It is also alarmingly insufficient, a hollow charade that won't bring either party what they believe that they are bargaining for. At the very best, it can be the first small step towards a more useful outcome; at its worst, it is makeup over a cancerous mole.

If we are to consider the idea of reparations as a form of reconciliation, we must first recast its definition in order to make it useful and constructive. The stated objective of reparations must be the reduction or elimination of the generational damage done by a systematic application of discrimination, and to provide a foundational balance for Black Americans to fully participate in a shared nation's present and future. Any accepted definition of the word reparations must encompass all of that, or else it must be rejected.

In searching for a definition that I could identify with, I began with the word reparation itself. As I expected, many of the first definitions that I found were too limited and unhelpful to my purposes. Wikipedia refers to reparations as the following:

***"Reparations for slavery** is a political justice concept that argues that reparations should be paid to the descendants of slaves."*

My discomfort with the concept of monetizing the atrocities of slavery is not based on some denial that it is deserved but rather arises from a pair of competing calculations: first, that any allocation that accurately equates the pain and suffering to dollars is incalculable (and therefore inadequate) and second, that the idea that "only" the direct descendents of American slaves have faced that sort of pervasive imbalance and obstruction is indefensible and incomplete.

If a serious resolution to the historic and current imbalance is to have meaning, it must recognize and respond to all of the history of racially motivated and legislated circumstances of denial and deprivation.

The particulars of the various published suggestions for reparations based on compensation for slavery's atrocities confirmed my sense of insufficiency. Various scholars, attempting to quantify the unquantifiable, have suggested numbers for distribution ranging from a few hundred dollars to as much as $80,000 or more. These are based on various permutations of some mathematical calculation of valuing slave labor, its economic impact and the abandoned promises compounded over a few hundred years, divided across 40 million or so recipients.

I consider these proposals to be irrelevant. To my sensibilities, it feels more like a poor excuse of an apology than a functional satisfaction of centuries of malicious restraint. Even if an $80,000 grant were provided to every Black family -- an amount that would likely represent between $750 billion and $1 trillion in federal provisions -- it would only represent a temporary relief, a one time salve spread over an unhealed and infected wound. A generation from now, would the impact of that single payment create a meaningful change in the opportunities and experiences of Black Americans in a still white preferenced society? I can mathematically calculate that diminishing impact, and it is neither determinative nor transformational.

Another definition of reparation might be more useful; Webster's offers this:

"..the act of making amends, offering expiation, or giving satisfaction for a wrong or injury.."

The act of making amends, if interpreted carefully, opens a larger door. Satisfaction cannot be achieved, amends would be insufficient, so long as the offense continues forward and is unresolved. The stopping of one man from beating another is of little value if (a) the beaten man is not healed, and (b) the offender is allowed to continue the abuse. Appropriate resolution cannot exist in the absence of systemic reprogramming and the recalibration of disadvantage and constraint. In that possibly contorted sense, the term reparations begins to apply to a meaningful discourse.

The majority of definitions offered by various sources and reference books appear to focus more on the application than the concept, suggesting an outcome (payment of cash as a response to transgressions) more than an objective (Resolution? Apology? Repair? Recompense?).

Without understanding the constructive purpose of reparations, the concept is hollow, without a mechanism for transforming, or even ultimately assessing its success or failure. It is only in understanding the objective that the manifestation takes on meaning.

For my personal purposes and efforts, I settled on the following as an initial definition for guiding my research and framing my suggestions:

Reparations are the collaborative effort to effectively redress historical and present transgressions, and to establish the foundation for a more equitable future.

The key words are important here.

Collaborative, because no meaningful solution can reasonably be imposed, so the solutions must be the process of a shared agenda and mutually accepted outcome.

Effort, because it will be a process rather than an event, one which will be long and difficult.

Effective, because success should be evaluated by the measurable applications and results rather than the political, theoretical or academic.

Redress, which, when defined as "the setting right of what is wrong", speaks to a common acceptance of the past and the present state of "wrongness".

Foundation, because reparations can and must serve as the base for continuing elevation and balancing, and a material resistance to any repeat of the transgressions once resolved.

Equitable, because the objectives are for the establishment of ongoing fairness and balance rather than simply punishment or profit.

There is another term that needs to be dealt with at this time. In the discussions of racial inequality, the phrase "affirmative action" is frequently denigrated and used as a polarizing political meme. It is often portrayed as a form of charity. It is periodically defended by a complicated insistence that it is not predatory towards white Americans, and a series of accompanying linguistic contortions.

This distinction is critical: the idea of reparation is not charitable. It is not something given by white America to Black Americans as a token. Reparations, as defined in this paper, are the steps necessary and appropriate to begin the process of repairing centuries of systemic deprivation and denial. As such, the projected outcome would be the elevation of the capacities and productivity of a major segment of our population, a discernible benefit to all Americans and to the nation as a whole.

To the degree that the programs discussed herein appear to preference Black Americans over white Americans, whether in terms of resources and opportunities, that appearance is intentional and factual.

As noted frequently, the historical and present conditions of Black life in America are indisputably disfavored; reconciliation of those circumstances requires addressing the various aspects of that imbalance. This in turn would require either elevating the conditions of Black Americans or denigrating the conditions of white Americans in order to level the playing field meaningfully. In my proposals, I have somewhat logically chosen to elevate.

In doing so, it is my fervent belief that the inevitable outcome would be the elevation of all Americans, and of America itself.

CHAPTER THREE

Evolution

We enter the world empty, without preference or bias. Immediately, we learn to value the touch of our mother, and from there to prioritize people and environments based on their provision of affection, safety and support. As our awareness expands, we come to accept as educators a variety of sources: familial, structured, proximate and ultimately, glowing on screens in front of us.

For too many, our education ends there. We are uncritical, happily accepting what we have already learned regardless of the origins. We are comfortable, preferring to hold on to biases that preference us, or that support our existing understandings. In the current world, we are able to surround ourselves with only confirmation, never challenging our beliefs or ourselves.

If we are fortunate, if we are still open to it, there are times when events or exposure forces open our eyes, demands that we get up from our soft couches of ignorance and complacency, and enter the working fields of awareness and responsibility… perhaps even a form of enlightenment.

For much of America, indeed the world, this is such a time relating to the depths of systemic racism in our society. Despite my prior belief that I understood, this has been such a time of evolution for me.

Reparation is a subject that I've thought about, read about and discussed with those close to me, but that I never felt that I had permission to write about. It always felt intrusive, like opining on the affairs of another couple, or suggesting answers to another person's faith. It felt as if I was intruding on someone else's problems, something having little or nothing to do with me.

It has been this moment, this explosive time in our society's growth pains, that has finally released me. It has helped me to understand that this is my personal problem, my cause. It is that awareness that frees me to fully engage, to offer thoughts towards its solution, because I now finally recognize that I am as much a participant in, and cause of, these systemic realities as anyone else.

My evolving beliefs begin with a basic premise: the wrongs that have been committed are not an event, but a trajectory that began in important ways far before the "original sin" of slavery in America over 400 years ago and one that continues to this day. The nature of man that leads one group to exert dominion over another has likely existed before history could record it. It has been the basis of all of our political systems; it has emerged as an outcome of our wars; it has defined how we exercise our religions. It is endemic to our species, and it persists in countless forms today.

That it is omnipresent does not make it acceptable or right, it merely helps us to recognize it, and to give it a name when we encounter it. A "benevolent dictator" is an oxymoron, and an impoverished excuse; by the very term, it is an exercise of dominion that is beyond the choice or effect of the subjected. Regardless of intention, according to the values that we profess as a society, it is unequivocally wrong. In our founding documents, we profess to pursue the governance by the consent of the governed; in our forefathers' early adoption of slavery, we mocked our own ideals and stated promises.

It is here that the first conundrum exists when we discuss reparations. To many whites, the concept of reparations is deemed a misplaced punishment for inexcusable and immoral actions taken by people long dead, an assault to others who are also beyond our present help. Like many families such as my own, there are no ancestors on either side that were present in this country when slavery existed. Nor did any of my ancestors benefit from the exploitation of slave labors and blood in America; my genealogy traces back fairly recently to various areas across Europe, as does the family of my wife. The different transgressions of our ancestors are well documented. To accept a personal punishment for American slavery — even on its most superficial terms — could feel arbitrary and inappropriately punitive.

It is that disconnect that has made reparation feel distant, as if it is more appropriately a private argument between the descendants of slave owners and the descendants of slaves. It has appeared as a battle that is not mine nor my children's, but I accepted that there was a logic to that limited premise for those others. When I've thought about it at all, it's never been to try and understand it's validity, but rather to passively consider the challenging logistics involved in the required genealogy. Surely, it couldn't apply to me…

And yet, I now clearly understand that I am complicit, and that there are scales that need balancing in the present day. The present transgressions and the undeniable presence of systemic inequality give credence and urgency to reparations. It is, and properly should be, on me and mine to address the imbalance in the foundation of our current nation; it is that revelation that informs and demands a present response.

When I say that I am complicit, it is a complicated confession. Like many others — although not nearly enough — I strive to be open to and aware of the feelings and stories of all of my neighbors and fellow travelers. I am sincerely repulsed by those around me that deny the humanity and pain of others. I accept and believe that the God that I follow has created all of His many hued children in His likeness; and if I truly believe that I see the countenance of God in everyone, how can I not love them? The broad diversity of my own beloved family — both blood and chosen — has led to angry defenses and spirited denunciations on its collective behalf. My ego has allowed me to believe that I am not a racist for those reasons, and my close personal relationships have included a broad gamut of good people that have supported that self delusion.

Regardless of whether or not that label of racist applies to me (and I fully accept that it does) I had never recognized the deeper history and present realities of Black life in America. With that willful obliviousness has come a lack of reaction and action, a paucity of indignation and rejection. The dialog of today has been in many ways revelatory, as it has at every turn begun an education that is far too long overdue, and inexcusably absent from my own. I knew of slavery, and the myriad atrocities perpetrated in its cause… but I did not understand or consider the profound impacts of racial inequity in the economic development of our country before and after emancipation, let alone today. I knew of the Jim Crow constrictions academically, and the visceral depravity of lynching in our nation… but it never occurred to me, as a self-described economist, to equate those denied rights and oppressions to the pervasive imposition of generational poverty and denied opportunity.

I can effectively project economic impacts forward for decades, but I failed to consider those same equations looking backwards, never applying their obvious conclusions to the present case. I had that ability, but I had never used it before now. Once I did, those calculations became critical and inescapable… and it placed a visual in my mind that I cannot shake.

I keep imagining a hundred yard dash, where the starting blocks of one runner are placed twenty yards closer to the finish line. The gun fires, and both runners leave their respective starting gates at the same time… but for the further back runner to win will require a miracle. Every now and then, a slow runner will be caught by an amazingly fast one, but if the two are even remotely comparable, the outcome is a foregone conclusion.

In understanding that imagery, I also understand that I have always been in that advanced position;

regardless of my role in placing down those blocks, I never stood up and either moved back, or called forward the other runner. I never demanded that the race be made fair, that we both start at the same point. I simply accepted my position, and ran my own race.

The concept of reparations, in my mind, is an acknowledgement that I now choose for the contest to be made fair, to insist that every one of us start at the same point. Belatedly, I disavow the advantage, and decry the unearned penalty conferred on my behalf against my fellow Americans. I agree to provide the other runner the benefits that I received from winning the rigged races, and accept that such equalization will be taken from my own purse.

Once we allow for reparations to be as much (or even more) about fairness than as a form of punishment, as much about the starting point of Black America vis a vis that of white America, the conversation changes radically. Those considerations incorporate not just slavery, but issues that have persisted far beyond it in innumerable ways. The arguments often made that every immigrant or minority population endured antipathy fails utterly when considering that the actual laws of the land — rather than some temporary societal dictates — specifically and persistently precluded one race from participation.

For hundreds of years, white Americans were free to build equity, to garner educations, to participate in the largess of a bountiful nation, while Black Americans — regardless of their legal status at the time — were not. When there was grudging provision granted by the government, white society often exacted their own retractions violently.

Acknowledging that history, the present reality where the average Black family has one tenth the wealth of the average white family represents not a difference in personal capability, but the reflected variance in their respective starting points and the continuing differences in the composition of the tracks being run on. For some white families, the advantage is a generational accrual of property and wealth, a feat not just more difficult but actually impossible for most Black families to have accomplished. For many Black families, disadvantages are the inevitable products of imposed cyclical poverty tracing back multiple generations. For many white families, it is an only slightly more subtle advantage, perhaps a familiarity with higher education and an address where the available free education was radically superior.

For every white family, it has been and remains a society where there are nominal restrictions, few inhibiting elements creating obstacles to their individual progress; for every Black family, it has been and remains the diametric opposite. Another image persists here: the nature of fish.

For many species of fish, the ultimate size of the individual fish is determined by the size of the tank that they are kept in; a certain fish in a ten gallon tank might grow to a few inches while the identical fish in a hundred gallon tank would grow to ten times the size. It is not the internal capacity of the fish, but the imposed environment that constrains its growth.

Similarly, in nature, some fish living in the presence of constant predators are commonly assumed to be smaller in size; when introduced to waters free of predation, the same fish grow to be enormous. Ask a Texas fisherman about alligator gars, and you'll hear tales of huge beasts lurking under bridges; ask an Everglades fisherman, and he'll describe an interesting but much smaller fish common to Florida waters.

Black families have been consigned to the smallest of fish tanks for virtually their entire presence in America, regardless of how or when they arrived. To assume that they would grow to their full size is to deny the power of environmental constriction. Black businesses have faced predators of every nature and origin — official, societal or white hooded — that have rarely hunted for white businesses. To assume that the free market was free for them is to deny the prevalence and impact of sanctioned predation.

To consign these constrictions only to history, to assume the disparate starting points as irrelevant relics of the past is to deliberately ignore the demonstrable realities of the present. Black America has been deprived of the economic and educational foundations taken for granted by white America, and continues to exist in a constrained environment that fights against their natural growth. For America to be what it purports to be, the scales must finally be balanced to the degree that it is currently possible to do so. For America to be its best, the walls of the tank must be shattered entirely.

The only reasonable mechanism for addressing the perpetuated disadvantages, the pervasive constrictions that have for practical purposes fulfilled the slander of intrinsic inequality, is to first attempt to replace what was taken away. To compensate without a prior recalibration is to offer a bribe in hopes for a pardon of a capital offense. If we consider a system of repayment as a singular moment in time, an event, then we are ignoring the undeniably valid premise of generational damage; a true response must be transformational, and effective in moving racial equality forward.

The starting blocks for the race must be averaged forward, even if that demands for a period of time that the advantage previously held by white Americans is reversed. There is too much to catch up, and it won't happen in a single race, no matter how wide the margin of victory is. The enduring result of reparations must be an uninterrupted future of fair starts, and a guarantee of evenly smooth tracks for everyone to run on.

There are any number of complex and controversial issues in any effort to create programs that will impact an entire segment of society, and the following suggestions are obviously not immune. For every proposal there is unquestionably a lurking problem, for every new program there are a dozen reasons why it cannot be done. That will always be so, but to move in this vital direction, the process must have a solid start.

There must be something tangible provided to establish an inaugural standard for others to consider, to attack and defend; that position must present a governing logic that at least resists invalidation. In the provision of such a starting point, the movement gains a foundation to push against in the effort upwards.

CHAPTER FOUR

Laying The Foundation

In the construction of anything intended to matter, to last, a good builder understands that without a solid foundation everything above ground will be compromised, and ultimately fail. So, it must be with the approach to reparations; it must come from a groundswell of Americans understanding the history of transgressions, acknowledging the critical need for redress, and accepting the validity of a proposed response.

Premature efforts to force acceptance of terms and conditions by a minority will indeed fail, and in falling short cause regression. This moment in time has demonstrated the potential for education and endorsement, as a majority of all people have found at least a temporary agreement in the exposed realities. That opportunity needs to be built on with a diversity of confirmation and an urgency of action, aggressively protected and consistently expanded on.

If you value the harvest, prepare well the soil for the seed...

The arousal of a nation, repulsed by the graphic exposure to another in the line of atrocities against Black Americans, has engendered historic protests and demands for change. Such dynamic moments in time create fissures in what were previously walls, cracks through which we can see new lights. That light shines this time, and we can leverage those cracks to begin a dialogue previously denied.

For all of the movements of the past decades, the subject of reparations has been considered too extreme for open discussion, much as the phrase Black Lives Matter was first murmured rather than shouted, and much the way that LGBTQ rights were once the province of only college campuses before they reached the mainstream. Times change, and awareness and acceptance sometimes catches up, often unexpectedly, and too often too late, but… sometimes.

I hold that the critical first step is for this subject to be raised not only as a Black demand, but as a white insistence, a matter of white conscience. So long as the most articulate voices for reparations are coming from "only" Black voices, no matter how thoughtful and persuasive, the entrenched "us versus them" mentality will seek to diminish their cause as self-aggrandizement. It is in the inclusion of numerous supportive white voices alongside those Black voices that will denature that argument, at least to those capable of being reached.

Another crucial step is for a massive surge in national education. The BLM movement has offered a critical teaching moment about the deeper, darker and more granular elements of Black history. It has been truly compelling. For many years, I had shared the Cornerstone Speech with friends and associates as if it were some secret, sheltered Rosetta stone insight into the Confederacy. In the past few months, I have seen it referenced in the national media countless times, to where white commentators now casually refer to it as if they'd been quoting it forever. They have not.

As a non-native Texan, I heard annual stories of the massacre and burning of Black Wall Street; in the past month, my lack of any true understanding of the scale and scope of the atrocities has become embarrassingly clear. It seemed that each week brought another reference point that exposed my ignorance. The shameful list goes on, and it needs to go much further, with much more light shined on it.

My own education was accrued in the supposedly liberal bastions of the northeast, during the 60's and 70's when young people and college students were considered radically in the vanguard of the civil rights movement. I learned literally nothing there of what I've since come to understand about the history of race in America that would be out of place in some comic book adaptation; I assume that the same applies to most Americans. The stories, the images, the sounds and feels of not just slavery, but of every generation since the physical shackles were broken need to be omnipresent, and permanent. Those lessons need to break free from the Smithsonian's impressive Black History Museum, and march across the street into the "regular" halls. We must no longer allow our nation to separate the history of racial animus from the history of America; it must be intertwined in our schoolbooks and our exhibits as intimately and inextricably as it has been in reality.

Once the calls for reparations are as diverse as we are; once the nation is confronted with the all-too long submerged stories and images of our true heritage; once the textbooks and museums begin to acknowledge their own sins of omission and lead the public revealing, then the movement towards reparation will have a critical mass behind it. The present moment may be sufficient to ignite the majority of that change, but the remaining challenge is imperative and presently unaddressed.

The litany of predicates above appears to suggest that this vital conversation is for some time well into an uncertain future. I strongly disagree. The requisite steps -- diversity of support, expansion of awareness, inclusion of the hard realities in our national telling of our history -- are in parts newly present, and their unfilled balance is not beyond our grasp. The "critical mass" is not yet present on this specific subject, but that is possibly more of a result of the lack of informed understanding than it is of a popular rejection. Much like any number of current social justice memes, the phrase "reparations" conjures up different images in every mind; in the absence of coherent definition and supporting logic, the inevitable result is an unhelpful hodgepodge, promoting reflections of internal fears, latent prejudice and misunderstanding.

The establishment of a national willingness to acknowledge and commit to an attempt to resolve past atrocities is essential and irreplaceable. Reparations that provide a meaningful and transformative outcome will require an unprecedented effort on the part of the entire country; without that motivation coming from a place of conviction, an inherently resistant democracy will inevitably defeat its own best angels. There is no shortcut; every skipped step will be painfully revisited until it is completed.

Even the most adamant voices for reparations struggle with quantifying the specific nature of its expression. It is referred to in abstract, as if words like substantial and equalizing represent a definable amount. They do not.

I accept that there might be different and concurrent conversations regarding some specific transgressions. One that is often referred to in this sense is Special Field Order No. 15, a signed promise made by General Sherman in January of 1865 (and subsequently rescinded by President Jackson later that fall) for "40 acres and a mule." pertaining to designated lands in South Carolina. I suggest that agreement and similar challenges are a separate, legalistic and perhaps unresolvable discussion. For these purposes, I prefer to focus on addressing the overriding offenses, past and present.

The map to meaningful and achievable reparations can be better found in what they are (or should be) intended to resolve:

The intentional and legislated deprivation of an entire race of their entitled humanity, and as a byproduct, their deprival of the range of material advantages and personal opportunities available to much of the rest of America.

It is these expropriations that have served as one of the fundamental millstones around the necks of Black Americans, one that has never been relieved and rarely sufficiently acknowledged.

To appropriately address the issue of reparations then requires not a single action, but a comprehensive and coordinated patterning of responses. As noted previously, I would opt for elevation of the historically oppressed to resolve the intrinsic disparities, rather than the diminution of the rest, in order to approach and achieve balance.

There is a universal benefit of rectifying these inequities in that the process will yield the best possible country for all to share, an outcome that suggests for the first time in our history that every person in America has an honest and unimpeded access to reach their individual potential.

I submit that any sincere effort needs to include an accounting in a broad aggregation of areas, specifically including education, housing, business, employment, health, voting rights and representation, social justice and social services. These pillars have been denied Black society by practice and statute, while for white America they have formed the basis for various levels of accrued wealth, health and status.

It is also critical to understand that those categories are inextricably intertwined, the historical denial of each providing support for the deprivations of the others. Only in providing a full and appropriate balance in all of these areas, will there emerge a path forward that will support Black Americans in equalizing any percentage of that staggered start.

One additional consideration is that, despite the pervasive obstacles and arbitrary constraints, a substantial and growing Black middle and upper class -- not to mention the expanding number of Black entrepreneurs and professionals -- have succeeded financially, rendering an exclusionary focus on the lowest socio-economic targets for any program unwarranted. Therefore, there must be specific accommodations that serve to benefit all economic classes of Black Americans in meaningful ways.

The suggestions that follow incorporate all of those critical pillars, and assume the existence of that necessary national will. It will offer a preliminary replacement (at least for the majority of America) of the flimsy questions "why" and "if" with the consequential questions of "what" and "how".

CHAPTER FIVE

Structure and Organization

We must accept that reparations are a process rather than an event. As such, supervision and management of that effort is critical, as the organic energies of formation give way to the mundane grind of implementation.

The physical manifestations of appropriate reparations will touch virtually every aspect of the national economy and society to differing degrees. The expression of such an expansive initiative must come out of a centralized authority, one without distraction or dilution of its core mission.

There is little to be gained by reinventing the wheel, much to be said for simply spinning it in a different direction. The present organization of our government and the directives of its agencies provide sufficient models and entry points for the creation of a new Department, one with the enduring mandate of fairness and racial equality. We have created far more with far less of a purpose.

Any comprehensive approach to reparations as a mechanism for a recalibration of racial inequality will need to impact virtually every aspect of our society, our economy and our government. It will need to coordinate a range of programs and policies adroitly, and to do so in a dynamic way that responds to organic changes in the field, to observed results and data, and to unanticipated circumstances.

No single legislation or program can reasonably succeed in crossing so many lines of administration and control. True reparations will require a defined objective that is expressed through a central agency, one that can reach into each area and collaborate towards modification and implementation.

The effective development and management of these programs and policies will require an unprecedented data collection and management initiative, logistically sophisticated and spanning financial, operational, social, enforcement and survey based inputs from across the country. This effort would be necessary in order to make the programs and policies responsive and efficient.

The primary and logical extension of these requirements would be the creation of a new governmental agency, which I will refer to (in a placeholder fashion) as the Department of Racial

Equality ("DRE") for the purposes of this discussion. That agency would have a clearly defined and articulated mission and, ideally, a future winding down to where it would eventually complete certain of its structural objectives and adjust as appropriate.

It would need to be housed within the Executive Branch, since the individual agencies that it would primarily work with -- Treasury, Health and Human Services, Homeland Security, Justice, Education, Commerce and Housing and Urban Development -- are located within those auspices. It would appear to justify a designated cabinet level representation, since it could not comfortably fall within any single agency given its reach and scope.

The mandate of that agency would include, but not be limited to, the following functions:

- To define and mandate the establishment of the various programs and policies within their designated agencies.
- To collect, manage and distribute a critical database related to the circumstances affecting racial justice as well as the operational results of the various programs.

- To establish and publish the specific targets, logistics and guiding metrics for each of the programs to be instituted.

- To recommend incremental adjustments and modifications to program operations and management, both internal and external, based on its data, information, analysis and observations.

- To consolidate financial costs and benefits, and to coordinate with Congressional leadership regarding the necessary annual appropriations.

- To oversee compliance, and to support the Justice Department in identifying and evaluating operational abuses and corruption within the programs.

- To adjust existing program targets and resources based on unanticipated circumstances and changing economic cycles.

- To author and promote legislative policies that will advance the continuing objectives of the agency and its constituents.

- To promote public awareness and information regarding program intentions and results, particularly their accrued benefits not only to the Black community, but to the national interests.

The formation of the DRE agency would require an act of Congress, which would allow for the national discussion to have a cohesive point of initiation for action. That formulation would also create a natural transition allowing for the staggered implementation of what will be a complex array of programs with varying impacts.

The duration of effective reparations will, by its nature, extend over a considerable number of years. Over that time, the circumstances surrounding the process will change substantially and to a large degree unpredictably. Having a specific agency empowered to calibrate and manage the various programs and initiatives would allow for necessary adjustments during periods of recession or depression, of war and peace, of prosperity and growth.

The practical effect of the construction of a Department of Racial Equality will be the efficient management and coordination of the necessary works, and the delineation of the resulting outcomes. The aligned benefit will be to demonstrate a global leadership in reconciliation, and to rebrand the U.S. as the preeminent force for racial equality. The benefits of that identity would be numerous, and would justify and assist America in the promotion of our international influence in matters of human rights and democracy.

The application of resources and the implementation of programs, whether derivative of federal, state or municipal governments, would require extensive logistics for localized distribution and maintenance. Rather than creating dedicated outlets for administering reparations, the major funding would be better used to reimagine the national network of social service offices as productive neighborhood centers for both input and output of resources and information.

A broad distribution of properly oriented, funded and staffed neighborhood facilities would allow for not only the effective dissemination of resources, but for a far deeper acquisition of critical data for informing ongoing program development and management. The integration of DRE programming into facilities geared to centralize provision of such constructive elements as limited health services; vocational education and counseling; recreation; child, senior and after school care; dispute resolution and localized advocacy. In doing so, these centers would contribute to the stabilization of neighborhoods and help to facilitate the process of seeking and providing assistance.

While there are many allocations and programming that need to be specific to the Black community, in every regard where possible such resources must be integrated into general improvements for all affected Americans. Without such integration, the act of providing and managing reparations will serve to further divide culturally rather than broaden through equalization. It is also important to project and pursue the movement towards recalibration (or even obsolescence) of the components of DRE programming as objectives are approached, then achieved. Through that wider and more inclusive application, important infrastructure will endure and thrive as balancing is gradually approached.

This highlights a critical consideration that must be built into the mechanisms of transformation. The applications of DRE, and increasingly the general provisions of government, must be actively projected as a positive process rather than a forced one, both for the benefit of the individual and for the community. To the degree that these expanded facilities can be seen as assets rather than impositions, the necessary elevation of all challenged classes of Americans can be destigmatized, promoting greater access and participation. In addition, the concentration on their positive contributions will allow the locations of these enhanced facilities to reduce or reverse their present negative impact on neighborhood perception and property values, a critical consideration to public acceptance.

There is one important consideration to the naming convention for the new Department, and a clarification. In this proposal, the solutions suggested are driven by a response to the systemic racism and abuses as they apply specifically to Black Americans.

Shamefully, American discrimination and bias has taken any number of forms, impacting multiple ethnicities, religious beliefs, national origins, sexual orientations and races. Even that list doesn't address bias based on gender, age or disability; the concept of "other" has always incorporated a majority of American citizens, often shifting historically with the times and with events.

The particular focus of the Department of Racial Equality in addressing Black issues has its genesis in two critical facts: first, that the predation on Black Americans has been specifically interred in the laws of the land, a level of official imposition that has been rarely attained by any other race. Secondly, the scale of the afflicted population is enormous, and can only be effectively addressed by a focused federal initiative.

Within that understanding, please note that several of the proposed programs will elevate entire socio-economic classes, with the primary benefit to Black

Americans coming from their disproportionate representation. To the degree that other classes of Americans are deprived of their fair participation in our nation, those can be addressed specifically and through expansion of programs such as those suggested here.

I'd also like to note a common misperception here: Hispanic is not a race. For too many years, it has been suggested as if it were, allowing a not-so-subtle inclusion of those Americans in the category of what too many consider "other". The current climate exacerbates that discriminatory aspect, and programs to address those prejudices are appropriate and sorely needed. The same has been occasionally done with Jewish Americans as well as various nationalities from time to time; the present treatment of Muslim Americans resembles racism as well in terms of the impact and pervasiveness.

Races that actually are recognized in America include white, Black, Asian, native (and Alaskan) and Hawaiian American. There is an existing agency for Native Americans (the Bureau of Indian Affairs) that will hopefully adopt the more applicable policies of the DRE for their own purposes. Statistically, Asian Americans provide little evidence of systemic racism in their social and economic participation; there is no doubt of substantial bias in many social and public contexts, but the urgent need for systemic correction is not obvious. If that appearance proves false, or if circumstances change in the future, then the DRE should be uniquely able to address it through their practices and resources; that capability should be included in its charter and formation.

CHAPTER SIX

Poverty and Context

The pride that America takes in its self-definition as the most powerful, wealthy nation in the history of the world is frequently exploited by politicians and advertising executives. It is a trope that is so commonly stated as to be unquestioned, and compared to any number of other identities, a relatively harmless conceit.

How then to explain the tens of millions of Americans oppressed by abject poverty, denied their share of that great and historic wealth? Do we ascribe it to chance, to some temporary misfortune, to some great sin committed that makes their affliction fair and deserved?

In the case of the poverty of Black Americans, we have a simpler, and more direct connection: the origins of their forced arrival, the laws of this land, the dictates of society, and the practices of our institutions have specifically forced that condition disproportionately on one eighth of our nation.

Reparations must address not only the historical impacts, but the derivative causes of present conditions in order to truly address the damage done, and presently felt.

The myriad deficits that are all too present in the lives and wellbeing of Black Americans are a present day manifestation of historical deprivations. The majority of the programs being advised here address those deficits going forward, but for too many the inflicted damage requires a more immediate remedy. Cyclical poverty, substance abuse, endemic health concerns, educational and vocational deficits and social disruption have disproportionately impacted the present community of Black Americans of virtually every generation.

Cycles of generational poverty within the Black community provide a clear vision into a deliberately disadvantaged past, and its irrefutable impact on the present day. It is important to realize that the Emancipation was only roughly five generations ago; the Civil Rights Act was just two generations back. Any genuine opportunity for Black Americans to build on a prior generation's success has been actively denied until just recently.

When white Americans think about those racial disadvantages, it too often feels removed, only a historical footnote. It was, in fact, yesterday… and in too many ways, today. A personal reference point:

I was born in 1956. I am just now a senior citizen, and yet it was almost a decade after my birth that Black Americans were able to vote throughout America. I was in grade school when it became legal for Black Americans to marry white ones. I was alive, and old enough to have seen and read a legally permissible sign on a bathroom door -- or employment office -- saying "Whites Only". I was in high school when the civil rights movement was being violently contested throughout the South.

Black Americans of my age were born into a different world than I was culturally, legally, functionally and economically. The inequity of our beginnings cannot be overstated.

My father, the son of Italian immigrants in New York, built a small business after leaving the Army in the 50's, and provided for whatever our family needed. His upbringing and public education were stable, his own family's resources steadily improving throughout his home life. The loans and financial opportunities that he and his own family took advantage of for housing, education, health and business were largely unavailable to Black Americans. The tangible benefits that my father received from the GI bill and other federal programs were often denied to Black servicemen.

As the largely urban area that I was born into began to broaden demographically, my parents moved to the suburbs in order to place my brother and me into a better public school within a "safer" neighborhood. The town that we moved to, and the public schools that I attended, were almost entirely devoid of Black faces. I pursued the subjects that interested me, and augmented my education with some travel and whatever resources I could benefit from. When I moved on to college (as was always assumed by family, society and my schools) I was fully prepared, properly outfitted and given every opportunity to succeed. I met my wife in college, and we built a life together from a strong, unrestricted base.

It's imperative to point out that my family growing up was far short of wealthy. At our best, we were staunchly middle class, at our worst, below that level. That limited class status was fully sufficient for me to be so deeply preferred.

When I moved into the business world, my familiarity with business and broad education led me to Wall Street in 1980, where Black peers were again few and far between. When I became an entrepreneur, my family experience was critical to both my confidence and my capabilities. When my children were born, there were resources financial, experiential and educational for them to draw on. Family stability, both in our household and in the network of relations that could be accessed, was a constant.

Every structural aspect of my upbringing, education, resources and support would have been far more difficult, and in some critical ways impossible, for a Black American of the same age and period to emulate. I was deeply advantaged, and I had a reservoir of those advantages to pass on to my children.

Considered on a national basis, at what point in history were those circumstances commonly available to the children of any generation of Black Americans? We can draw lines from emancipation through to the present time, and we can see that the grudging, erratic advancement has never allowed for the type of familial succession that white Americans take for granted. For the preponderance of that period, such accumulation of advantages was specifically denied by federal legislation, and common and local law; for the rest, it was (and is) constricted by societal and functional discrimination.

Any reparation of those denied advantages must include addressing the victims of those deprivations, the present day generations of Black Americans who were never given a fair chance to prosper. The traceable impacts include more than the critical ones dealt with elsewhere in this book, such as housing, education, business opportunity and social justice; they are manifest in a racial over-representation in the ranks of poverty, compromised health, substance abuse and mental illness. It is here that remedial programs, administered through dedicated outlets for these specific social services, are the appropriate and required prescription.

Poverty affecting a given generation of a family creates a distinct gravity back towards poverty in the next, through the absence or inefficiency of individual or collective safety nets and the paucity of tools available to help elevate. While many Black American families found the means to escape the pull, it was always a challenge of a greater magnitude than any presented to white Americans. That disparity has led to the current statistical indictments where 22% of Black families currently live in poverty, defined as having a household income of less than $21,000 for a couple with one child. That percentage was prior to the pandemic's vast economic impact; present day statistics will be far more grim once fully updated.

Poverty of any form is a deeply complicated and fraught condition. The disparate causes of systemic poverty are often rooted in an evolved personal environment where circumstances have created obstacles that are difficult to treat collectively, or to align into convenient categories. In the absence of an existing base of foundational support, any disruption or crisis can trigger a dislodging of an individual or a family from relative economic stability into instability. Once the situation has so deteriorated, obtaining the tools and resources necessary to re-establish solvency can be too challenging to find and harness.

It is not possible, nor appropriate, to isolate the addressing of Black poverty from all other forms of poverty. The establishment of a successful system in proximity to others for whom those solutions are denied would be both dangerous and unproductive. Any emphasis on existing Black poverty would need to occur within an improved environment for all Americans, one that could provide the transitional aid and opportunities necessary to elevate an entire class of people. As noted, the far heavier weight of Black poverty means that any broadly applied solutions would have a disproportionately positive impact for Black Americans.

In constructively addressing poverty in any form, it is necessary to understand that the conditions of poverty fall into different categories. Poverty itself is not an identity. By definition, the most impoverished person can be immediately lifted out of poverty by the infusion of sufficient resources. Therefore, poverty must be understood as a product of specific circumstances, regardless of how complicated and intertwined the individual circumstances are.

In addressing systemic Black poverty, there is a need to identify a sequence of parameters, and to delegate resources and solutions accordingly. These parameters can be partly understood through a series of questions and answers:

Is the individual capable of sustaining themself under different and appropriate circumstances? In the event that they are not -- due to physical, mental or educational limitations -- then addressing their situation requires entirely distinct programs and resources than for those who have that capability.

Is the individual impoverished due to demonstrably temporary circumstances? If the reasons for the lack of economic stability is temporary, whether due to micro or macro circumstances, the nature and form of support would fall into different categories than in those for whom poverty is not temporary.

Is the condition of poverty significantly impacted by the current family structure? With increasing frequency, poverty is in large part driven by the presence of one or more dependants, whether children or elders, who are non-contributors to the household income. In Black families particularly, the absence of two wage earners where children are present is a substantial factor. According to some recent statistics, single parent households represent a majority, and perhaps as much as two thirds of all Black families.

It is only with proper identification that individual applications of resources and support can be appropriately determined. DRE programs for addressing poverty would need to include the following:

- Integration into and specific amplification of existing programs in disability, mental health and substance abuse that provide specific benefits to Black Americans.
- Specific development of external educational programs that can provide remedial and vocational advancement for Black Americans of all ages.
- Specific expansion of existing SNAP (Supplemental Nutrition Assistance Program, or food stamps) programs to focus on providing sufficient (rather than minimal) resources at appropriate levels of prenatal, childhood and senior nutrition.
- Transitional financial support for Black Americans who have lost their jobs, whether or not such employment qualifies under existing unemployment standards. Black Americans are disproportionately represented in industries (i.e. hospitality, retail, service, etc.) that have limited applicability to state unemployment

programs. Provision of this support should be integrated into existing program logistics.

- Transitional financial support for Black Americans during periods of general economic distress, specifically providing for the preservation of existing housing access and the acquisition of critical resources. As in other areas, the justification for this provision is the fundamental absence of reserves and generational support.

- Extensive provision of localized high quality child care, after school and elder care programs, facilitated by the expanded social service facilities envisioned. As in other areas, these programs should be available to all neighborhood residents based on a sliding income scale, with Black families initially at no cost, and transitioning to common participation as economic equality is approached.

These programs, in combination with the defined programs in housing, education and business, will offer a broad reconciliation of existing detriments and deficits. Further adjustments to these programs will be needed to address specific issues of Black rural poverty in both agricultural regions and specifically disadvantaged areas. As DRE data and information analysis develops further recommendations, implementation can be focused through the developed infrastructure or through direct applications.

CHAPTER SEVEN

Social Justice

At the very core of the original national sin of slavery was the denial of freedom to some human beings by others. In contravention of the dictates of our founding fathers, who professed that such freedoms came not from man but from God, generations of Americans chose to usurp that authority for their material advantage. Of course, so did those founding fathers…

The deprivation of freedoms – in every regard and expression of the term – did not end with Emancipation. It has persevered through every decade since, and remains a scourge for Black Americans today. It lurks inside of our institutions, particularly those involved in the management of the populace. It is counted in the disproportionate number of Black men behind bars, sent there because of an imbalance of enforcement and sentencing. It bursts out into the world through another killing of Black Americans by authorities of the state, graphic and undeniable.

Without social justice, there can be no true reparation for the sin of slavery, or for the enduring legacy of systemic racism. It is the cornerstone, the rock on which all redress must rest.

The intertwining of Social Justice and any programs for reparations is both essential and complicated. On one hand, the history of racial oppression and constraints has had a critical impact on the economic disparity and lack of opportunity present today. On the other hand, there are aspects to social justice that relate to socio-economic discrimination, and others that extend significantly beyond the impositions on Black Americans to those of other races and ethnicities. For these purposes, I'll assume that the prescribed responses will be primarily governed by the DRE, and that the resulting impact will be felt across the board.

This much is undeniable: there can be no effective outcome from reparations without a comprehensive addressing of systemic social injustice.

The issue of social justice has been at the crux of the enhanced public awareness and support presently experienced by the Black Lives Matter movement and its allied initiatives. Through visual evidence and media amplification, recognition of the atrocities perpetrated against Black Americans have become undeniable and for many, finally unacceptable.

Triggered by the breadth of the public protests, a national movement for the reform and reevaluation of police policies and structure is being undertaken from local precincts to the halls of Congress and the White House. A host of initiatives, from cosmetic to transformative, have been proposed and -- in far fewer cases -- enacted; initiating what promises to be the first period of significant change in generations.

Problematic to the implementation of change is the fragmented and uncoordinated nature of the challenges and related responses. Those difficulties are compounded by the diverse jurisdictions that govern the various elements of law enforcement. Federal powers only have limited impact, while below it disparate levels of authority from state to local government hold sway.

In this matter, the responsibilities of the DRE could be particularly useful, and potentially determinative. The DRE would create and distribute national guidelines for the structure and parameters of law enforcement agencies and enforcement policies. It would seek legislative authority to impose and confirm parameters across state lines. To the extent possible, the DRE would actively promote and motivate legislation on federal and state levels in accordance with its recommendations.

While enforcement of those guidelines could be problematic on levels other than federal, there are present tools available to the agency for influencing policies at lower levels. Much in the way that the Federal Highway Administration (FHWA) exerts some control over speed limits through the provision of certain federal construction and land acquisition funding, the DRE could coordinate its work with the Justice Department in order to withhold or promote certain pools of federal aid and to control access to non-essential programs where lower level agencies were recalcitrant.

More critically, the Defund the Police movement has brought to the fore a valuable concept for empowering structural changes, and the DRE would be the natural designated vehicle for motivating and implementing those adaptations.

Given the breadth of the DRE's influence across agencies, the reallocation of police force funding at the state and local levels could be oriented towards redirection into the newly developed community resources for use in mental health, substance abuse and addiction, housing and homeless programs, social services and dispute resolution, all in keeping with a set of nationally published guidelines. Uncooperative state agencies could be constructively motivated or punitively addressed based on the level of disagreement and the severity of the issues faced.

The unique data management function of the DRE would make it capable of designing individually optimized programs for municipal allocations and adjustments. By impacting the programs directly governed or influenced by the DRE that pertain to social issues, the agency could do more than simply advise; it could partner with the local government in applying existing federal funds and special appropriations, maximizing the resultant benefits for the affected areas.

The DRE would also be the natural repository of the national database for racial and other abuses by law enforcement officers, providing it to the Justice Department for publication or internal use as appropriate.

In addition to advising and motivating structural changes, the comprehensive database kept by the DRE would be useful in identifying and addressing local and national disparities in law enforcement and incarceration statistics. The agency would have the authority to demand and access information based on those disparities, and to provide notice and guidance to state

Attorneys General. In extreme cases, the DRE could motivate investigations by the Justice Department where anomalies indicated it was appropriate.

With adjustments to current instructions and policy, the DRE could also be empowered to trigger Justice Department Pattern or Practice investigations based on a preponderance of statistical evidence rather than awaiting the filing of requests or complaints by state Attorneys General.

The establishment of federal standards, with the ability to create and distribute supervisory and analytical evaluation tools, would promote best practices across the country and create a far more rapid response to identified and demonstrated areas of concern.

Another critical responsibility in the area of social justice would be in establishing and advocating policy and legislative actions relating to the present epidemic of Black incarceration. A painful remnant of generations of systemic racial bias in law enforcement and organizational practices, the preponderance of Black

American males in jail negatively impacts every aspect of the Black community at large.

Without question, much in the corrections industry is in a desperate and long overdue need of overhaul and reconstruction, from the contrarily motivated private prison system to the abusive labor practices. It is simply that the grievous overrepresentation of Black American males makes this an urgency appropriate to be dealt with as a particularly racial policy.

The disproportionate use of arrests and detention -- particularly in urban environments -- has long functioned as a mechanism for "controlling" Black Americans. It has long had crippling implications for a broad range of social ailments, resulting in artificially inflated levels of family disruption, chronic unemployment and cyclical poverty.

I am particularly persuaded by the insightful lines being drawn directly from American slavery through to the modern biases and practices relating to Black incarceration. In that light, the unequal application of enforcement and captivity appears as a societal clinging to racial subjugation, a stunningly obvious connection that eluded me completely prior to the present conversations. I suspect that much of America shares my ignorance. It is important for that to change as a critical function of the larger educational process.

There are a number of specific policies and programs that should receive immediate attention within the implementation of any program of reparations. They would include, but not be limited to, the following:

- A significant reduction or elimination of the use of incarceration for nonviolent minor offenses, to specifically include offenses related to drug use.

- The establishment and funding of more robust national programs for the support of and advocacy for individuals following the terms of their incarceration, to include transitional economic support and productive vocational programs.

- A significant reduction or elimination of the private prison industry. During the transition period, DRE could use data collection practices to ensure that the disproportionate effect of such facilities on Black American incarceration was not expanded.

- A significant reduction or elimination of unpaid or marginally paid prisoner labor.

Current practices have created a distortion where hundreds of major corporations benefit inappropriately from prison labor, presently valued at over $2 billion per year. In the event that prison labor was continued, it should be reorganized as a direct precursor to specific employment following release.

- A significant reduction or elimination of incarceration due to a demonstrated inability to pay bail on non-violent offenses. Cash bail is a process that disproportionately impacts Black Americans, and that specifically perpetuates and exaggerates the impact of excessive Black incarceration.
- A significant reduction or elimination of incarceration due to a demonstrated inability to pay such minor offenses as outstanding traffic or parking offenses.
- The elimination of felon voting disenfranchisement on a national basis.

In addressing social justice concerns, the DRE can and should be the home of critical data collection and policy advocacy. Using a more holistic approach than is common, DRE could firmly establish and publish direct correlations between the policies of confinement and their impact on social and economic development for the Black community. In creating that information, DRE would be an effective advocate and support for further policy recommendations and adjustments.

CHAPTER EIGHT

Voting Rights and Representation

We like to reference our democratic form of government as representational. That is a primary definition, that the collected individuals of America are represented by elected individuals who have their specific interests in mind, and who can be replaced when they fail to accurately understand those wishes.

If the validity of our government is derived from representation, then what is the power that it holds over those whom it does not represent, who have no authority to elect or to petition?

For most of the American experiment, Black Americans were specifically deprived of that fundamental right. In turn, the government did not represent their interests, ignored their petitions and gave dramatic preference to the white Americans that held the power of the vote.

Progress towards a critical objective is not the same as reaching it. In the present day, Black Americans are still being denied their rights to vote and for representation in their governance. While it is often through more subtle and obscure methods, the intention and impact is as undeniable as it is wrong.

Reparations without representation is the payment of a check without funds behind it. There is no reason to believe that it will clear, and little recourse when it doesn't.

One of the challenges to Black American participation in policy and governance is the historical restrictions placed on its representation, whether through outright preclusion, voter suppression or bias driven limitations. The Voting Rights Act of 1964, critically created to end such constraints, has too often been subverted by such practices and intents through to the present day. The reality is that too often, voting has been and remains more difficult, less accessible, and at times even dangerous for Black Americans, as multiple courts and organizations have attested to.

The recent adverse ruling by the Supreme Court on key parts of the Voting Rights Act in Shelby County v Holder ushered in another wave of adverse practices. While multiple courts have held that enduring issues such as limited poll access, racially engineered gerrymandering, shortened early voting periods and voter intimidation are evidence of illegal racial animus within the system, they continue broadly across America.

The critical equation is this: racial equality in any or all forms is dependent on equality in voter representation and active participation in governance. Without appropriate representation, advancement is too often driven by interests other than, and often adverse to, those of Black Americans. To compensate for existing and intentional disparities, the DRE must have a specific mandate to promote and advocate for Black American voter registration, voting and candidacies.

There are several areas where DRE should exert its influences or initiate policies.

In the matter of voter suppression, one of the primary functions of the DRE must be the development of, and advocacy for, legislative policies that protect voter rights and guaranteed poll access for Black Americans on a national basis. This will benefit all Americans regardless of race, but the practice of minority suppression is the trigger for reform. Where practical, DRE's database and analysis could be provided in support of litigation by governmental and private interests; in all regards, broad publication and public access of revelatory information would serve the objective of promoting equality.

A direct response to predatory practices has been difficult to initiate, monitor and enforce due to the distributed nature of state and local controls. Through its integrated database, DRE could identify and expose discrepancies in voter patterns and participation in local governance as they affect Black populations.

In instances where there are indicated suppression offenses, DRE would provide guidance and support to the appropriate divisions within the Department of Justice for investigation and prosecution. In the more likely event of generalized bias, DRE could engage its local facilities to promote and support voter registration, voter education and protection of polling area integrity through advocacy and even physical presence. This aspect of protection and preservation of access must be fundamental to the DRE mission.

In terms of Black participation in government, DRE would provide programs for the education and sponsorship of Black candidates on local and state levels, with the intention of expanding opportunities and representation. Such programs could incorporate specific training and coaching on application and qualification process, campaign management, media and self promotion, policy formation and fundraising, along with the provision of background data and information on constituencies.

Inevitably, it is likely that the program would be asked to provide financial support for Black candidates. This is particularly true where DRE analysis determines an acute geographic underrepresentation, or where demonstrable evidence suggests suppression or bias. It is conceivable that such support might take the form of materials, grants or organization of volunteer efforts, but any specific application of financial support could well be problematic on a number of levels, and would have to be the result of considerable organizational evaluation and care.

A difficult but critical component of DRE's involvement in educating and promoting Black American candidacies comes in the agency demonstrating a lack of preference in the ideologies and party affiliation of the entrants into its program. DRE must establish internal and transparent practices where eligibility and support is unquestionably determined solely on the basis of race. If there is any demonstrable extent to which the programs preference one party or ideology over another, the integrity of the entire program will be irredeemably compromised.

CHAPTER NINE

Education

In a culture where knowledge is acknowledged as power, the intentional deprivation of education is a means of oppression, a denial of access to the tools for economic or professional ascension.

Black Americans have been denied equal access to quality education consistently and presently. From earlier periods of absolute exclusion to current imbalances in critical resources (human, financial and physical) white America has benefitted from the best of a system that has been institutionally prejudiced and grossly distorted.

Reparations must create an equalized environment for the acquisition of those keys to power and wealth. It cannot allow historic deprivations to be represented in the current or future generations. The provision of other resources and tools through reparations, regardless of the sincerity of intent, are irrelevant if they are not supported by the knowledge of how best to use them.

Equal access to quality education is one of the essential and indispensable pillars of equality itself.

The history of racial inequality has included a deliberate and determined effort to ensure that Black Americans were not educated to the same extent and quality of white Americans. There is a discussion to be had as to whether racial segregation in schools has ever been fully resolved; I prefer the side that argues that it hasn't. The elevation of educational opportunities is a critical foundation to releasing Black youth to finally realize their fullest individual promise.

The reparation contribution to educational equality should include four distinct parts: a focus on pre-k, increased scholastic resources, expanded collegiate opportunities, and a mandated expansion of Black history in general education.

Quality pre-k education has been proven to provide a significant and calculable impact on future scholastic success. At present, the availability of public pre-k opportunities are wholly based on location, and on what each individual district has determined to provide. As of this writing, only three states -- Florida, Georgia and Oklahoma -- provide pre-k facilities through all of the public schools. Nationally, only 22 percent of all 4 year olds are eligible.

By focusing federal funds on the creation and development of high quality pre-k facilities, the benefits would accrue to all children, but be particularly valuable to Black families, where single parent homes are predominant. During the transition period as the system is developed, participation for Black children could be stimulated through grants and vouchers applicable to existing facilities.

It is particularly important that the developed facilities adhere to universal standards regardless of location. Any failure to create elevated minimum standards would potentially destine Black children to inferior facilities based on present demographics. This would exacerbate rather than eliminate the divide. As noted, the developed facilities must not be located or prioritized exclusively for Black children; that would perpetuate segregation that would be equally destructive.

The development of a superior pre-k education would provide a foundation for future educational success for all American children. The ability for Black American children to participate where they live would be a positive move towards eliminating existing socio-economic advantages.

In dealing with K-12 education, a substantial and federally legislated funding program towards the elevation of existing school systems is critical. That elevation must include the subsidization of higher teacher salaries and the establishment of substantially improved minimum standards for physical infrastructure and internal resources, is critical. By radically improving existing teacher and administration quality, infrastructure and resources, the pervasive segregation trends would materially ease. The existing incentive to actively avoid underperforming school districts would be largely reduced or eliminated. Sadly (and standing as a further indictment of the generational damage) a substantially disproportionate amount of underperforming and under-resourced schools currently serve minority youth.

An aggressive reduction in the existing chasm in quality education would be an important step toward resolving an out of balance developmental disparity by creating expanded educational opportunities for Black youth that have previously been denied.

Higher education is a hallmark of American success, considered essential to upper level incomes even as the costs have become inaccessible for far too many. The prospect of crippling debt often discourages those who might otherwise qualify, an aversion reinforced by the realities of income disparities in the workplace for Black graduates.

Here lies one of the more critical contributions to the movement towards equality that must be incorporated into reparations: for at least a sufficient number of years to encompass a pair of generations, the federal government should fully subsidize higher education for Black youth, to include advanced degrees. These subsidies must be unrestricted as to the college program selected.

The removal of financial considerations for higher education might prove the single greatest long term equalizer that can be employed. In conjunction with the superior preparation from pre-k through high school, the removal of financial barriers would help promote generations of young Black Americans to more fully realize their potential. This would result in their establishing a foundation of accomplishment that would assist in eliminating another portion of perpetuated white advantage.

One aspect of a greater inclusion of Black Americans in the ranks of higher education is subtle, but has an enormous impact. In almost all areas where higher incomes are found, networks are essential to advancement and mobility. These networks are primarily evolved in colleges and graduate programs, creating a barrier to success for those excluded. As more Black Americans participate and graduate, more will find access to those relationships, and the benefits derived.

In addition to the structural imperatives, it is essential that curriculums at all levels are adjusted to belatedly include the stories of racial injustice and predation. My own family has a portion of Jewish heritage; we have properly learned to insist on the trans-generational telling of the Holocaust as a cautionary tale, that no future generation should ever consider that the bloody stain of that crime will someday fade away; such it must be with the stain of not just slavery, but of the persistent inhumanity that preceded and followed it. In order to end that history (and to preclude its recurrence) we must first know fully of its existence, of the specific nature of its criminality and injustice.

History has indicated that the expansion of curricula cannot be left solely to the states. The DRE must achieve the authority to mandate and review minimal standards for content and language, or else the racial bias of the few members of state school boards will be enough to perpetuate national ignorance. Current law provides deference to states in their construction and supervision of curricula and resources. In light of that structural impediment, incentives such as subsidies in the cost of approved texts and support for conforming programs would likely be required, and would be appropriate given the benefits accrued.

CHAPTER TEN

Housing

Americans are not a nomadic people. We establish ourselves in specific locations, rooted in our neighborhood and safe in our private space. We choose where we live based on proximity to work, to worship, to communities that we prefer.

That is, unless we are Black citizens in America.

For them, the history of housing inequality is deeper and more sinister than it might appear. Since being freed from physical bondage, Black Americans have been consistently told where they are allowed to live without regard to their preferences. Inherent in the deprivation of economic resources, defined by institutional racism, Black citizens have been corralled into arbitrary boundaries by law and white society.

Once restricted to specific areas, white America was able to oppress Black Americans more directly, denying them quality resources such as education and protection, and applying law enforcement on an entirely biased basis. Access to the same financial products, opportunities and insurance as white Americans was withheld; critical infrastructure, transportation and even quality food supplies were sparse and poorly maintained.

Reparations must include a breaking of the barriers that have remained intact for far too many generations, and the explicit understanding that the establishment of a person's home, their engagement in a community is a choice that can never again be restricted by race.

A litany of the components of racial inequality are manifested in the housing equation. For virtually all of the Black experience in America, there has been a prevalent bias limiting (or eliminating) access to good housing in desired neighborhoods, availability of specific properties, and in fair bank financing and insurance. Critically, the biases that precluded Black ownership of property and homes has been an additional constraint on the accrual of generational wealth.

As a group, Black Americans have historically been forced to live where white Americans have told them to, in areas that are often deprived of services and basic resources, and that are subsequently over-policed and underfunded. The crime of red-lining, for too long in history not even a crime, meant that crucial financial terms, availability and conditions were disparate between the races, further stretching the divide.

The balancing of this issue is more complicated, but can be partially addressed by providing the tools for Black Americans to afford disproportionately better housing. For these purposes, the existing government backed Enterprise agencies (such as Freddie Mac and Fannie Mae) could be employed for the purchase side of the equation, providing a special class of loan availability that eases entry into the home ownership market. While the derived terms of that financing can reasonably be debated (including income levels for qualification) my initial suggestion would have the following characteristics:

- A federal grant in the amount of 10% of the purchase price, with such grant being repaid from the proceeds of the sale if the title holder does not live in the home for a minimum of 10 years (with exceptions for forced movement due to work, health or death) but forgiven beyond that time. Limits in the amount of this grant would be based on median housing values in the region. This grant would serve as the total downpayment for purchases, unless the purchaser chose to provide greater equity.

- Fixed interest rates subsidized at 0% for up to thirty years, depending on the buyer's choice of maturity. The combination of a down payment grant and the no interest loans would dynamically impact the level of housing available to Black Americans through an improved debt to income ratio, a determinative measure of buyer affordability that is a prime element of mortgage loan qualifications.

These provisions would allow a generation or more of Black Americans to acquire permanent homes at levels beyond their present capacities. In doing so, it would help offset some of the inherent disadvantages, and would simulate programs that were historically denied to Black Americans.

By increasing their potential buying power, Black purchasers would have greater freedom in choosing neighborhoods as well as quality and types of homes. The features of this program would significantly incentivize Black home ownership while the down payment grant terms would promote long term retention of those homes. Ultimately generating stability and active participation in neighborhood development.

For the population of renters, the solutions are somewhat limited but necessary. There would need to be two features — a grant that approximates a percentage of the rent regardless of the property or location engaged, and an allied program that would provide a safety net in the event of health or work interruptions. The latter feature is justified by the greater issues caused by historic inequalities in health and employment.

Conceptually, I would suggest that the grant portion of the program should attempt to reflect the percentage difference in area rents relating to historic Black neighborhoods and adjacent historic white ones. While further research on particular calculations is necessary and appropriate, the functionality is clear: the subsidized opportunity for Black Americans to break free of what have been intentional barriers to better living conditions, and at the base, to housing itself.

In addition to the grant program, a separate program for temporarily supporting Black renters in covering rent payments during health challenges or out of work periods is required. This program would acknowledge the disparities in current Black health circumstances, single parent households and consistent employment that are directly resultant of generational inequality. The program would be administered as adjuncts to existing disability and unemployment programs.

In all of these programs, it is critical that there not be a cap on the dollar value of the purchase or the rental, other than the specific financial qualifications of the individual or family. The objective is not only to lift the lower economic strata, but to enhance the quality of life for all Black Americans, regardless of their economic level. Just because a runner miraculously overcame their staggered start is not a reason for penalizing their accomplishment; they were as handicapped by the same circumstances as all Black Americans have been.

Dealing with the issue of disproportionate Black homelessness is crucially important. The programs for partially subsidizing rental costs would have an impact on some number of homeless individuals and families; expanded programs in mental health and occupational support would be relevant to others. The distributed neighborhood centers could be impactful on identifying and referring the homeless for support on a geographically relevant basis, and monitoring changes in that population.

Ultimately, homelessness itself -- a present scourge nationally -- requires a distinct and inclusive addressing from the federal government, through HUD and social services. That said, DRE would be the necessary originator of information and programming in addressing the particular impact on the Black community, and in coordinating continuing responses as changing circumstances dictate.

CHAPTER ELEVEN

Business

We are a capitalist country, founded on that principal and aggressively defensive of its tenets. We frequently equate money with power, and lead the world in consumerism and individual wealth. Our relationships across the globe are based on our unprecedented ability to create resources, and to barter them for obedience to our principals. Internally, we equate social status with wealth, and pass down what remains of our fortunes along with our names.

Within that economic system and those societal priorities, the deprivation of any citizen of the opportunity to create and amass wealth is a very specific form of oppression. That America has precluded Black Americans from sharing in this country's promise, has deliberately deprived Black Americans of their individual and collective potential, goes directly to the heart of what we believe that we are as a nation.

True reparations must openly acknowledge this transgression, and the responsibility of the nation to reform and provide compensation. The act of removing the barriers and adjusting the accounts for past constraints is an essential component of equality, and an undeniable obligation.

Fortunately, we are the self-acknowledged masters of the business world, and the curators of wealth. This should not be difficult.

The history of American entrepreneurs represents an irrefutable demonstration of Black engagement, talent and success. That same evidence reveals the subsequent predatory, exclusionary and too often violent reactions to burgeoning success by individuals, communities, society and legislative actions.

The ability to take an idea, to transform a passion from nothing into something that can feed a family or change a generation is a cornerstone of America's self identity. In terms of our economic dynamism, it is the simplest definition of who we believe we are. That fundamental dream has been aggressively denied Black Americans since the beginnings of our nation, and remains unfairly more complicated for them today. In providing a fundamental and specific facility for the support and development of Black business ownership, those scales of equality might begin to find some balance.

The recent machinations of the U.S. Treasury and the Federal Reserve in response to the economic impact of the Coronavirus pandemic offer some potential structures for useful credit facilities and programming.

The Treasury should establish and significantly fund an expansion of the existing Small Business Administration programs for the development and support of new Black owned businesses. Inherent in these enhanced programs should be greatly reduced barriers to qualification, internalized considerations for extending payments and refinancing, and an aggressive integration of the existing -- but rarely used -- resources for business education, compliance and development.

Coupled with these expansive lending facilities should be a curated federal grant program administered by the DRE and tied to both higher education programs and entrepreneurial proposals. The realities of capital acquisition for start up projects include a common reliance on network and familial funding, bringing the discussion back to the intentional deprivation of Black Americans of generational accumulations. In order to compensate for those systemic inequalities, the grant program would provide a useful (if only partial) simulation of prevalent white societal advantages.

The program that would best facilitate small business development would be access to risk capital at sustainable costs, because such capital is the most common barrier to project success and stability. Since providing capital without accountability or proper preparation is not constructive, the DRE could establish reasonably attainable parameters and distinct access points for entrepreneurs emerging from collegiate environments, from the workforce and from existing businesses looking to expand or revamp their operations in response to circumstances. These standards should be supported by programs to assist prospective entrepreneurs in attaining those qualifications. The combination of defined qualifying standards along with accessible and reasonably priced capital would be revelatory, and a massive boon to entry.

The DRE should be the gatekeeper to these programs, soliciting participation from the Black community, exposing graduates at all levels to the opportunities, and maintaining data and information on relevant matrices of success. The DRE should provide specific resources and support for the initiation and structuring of small businesses, primarily through a physical and educational presence located in the neighborhood centers. This would also be valuable in aligning business starts with area needs and relevance, a potentially significant factor in early success.

The support of new and growing endeavors, and the expansion of support for entrepreneurial pursuits on the part of recent graduates and operators will create a motivation for the necessary energy and effort of significant expansion. It will provide a critical momentum for Black business in establishing a greater presence in the American economy, and from there a greater global representation.

One further step in equalization would be for the Federal Reserve to maintain and potentially expand the scope of its Main Street lending facilities. These could focus in part on facilitating the transition of qualifying Black originated corporations from private to public enterprises.

Aside from the obvious function of creating highly visible role models and demonstrated opportunities, the emergence of greater representation of Black originated corporations in the public market would promote a number of critical outcomes, including but not limited to:

- The opportunity for significant blocks of capital and effective leverage to fall more frequently under the control of Black founders and chief executives.
- The practical development of more Black CEOs and other C-suite executive resumes, allowing for their expanded infusion through the broader corporate ranks.
- The heightened opportunities for directed investments of fund and program capital into Black originated corporations.

- The justification of greater participation in corporate Boards of Directors by Black executives and founders, and their subsequently increased influence on corporate direction.

As in almost all of these specific initiatives, the primary objective of the large business programs would be for them to taper down the more preferenced resources if and when the levels of Black participation became demonstrably more normalized. While there should never be a certain expiration date, if over time the programs are not creating the desired effects, they should be revisited and modified until they do. This should be particularly enforced in the matter of accessing large scale capital on a preferential basis. The DRE would be responsible for evaluating penetration and representation, and adjusting the targets and levels of funding accordingly in conjunction with the Federal Reserve and Treasury.

CHAPTER TWELVE

Health and Wellness

If you do not have your health, you have nothing.

In a nation that holds that statement to be self-evident, it is somewhat fitting that access to quality health care (and its supporting resources) is often directly correlated to individual wealth, status of employment and geographic location. In denying Black Americans all three of those prerequisites, we have systematically deprived them of the same health outcomes as white Americans have enjoyed, leading to graphic disparities in present day conditions. The Covid-19 pandemic forced those disparities into sharp relief, exposing the nation to the realities that have always existed, and still exist today.

Reparations must actively resolve the current health care discrepancies regarding access, conditions and support in order to address the deficiencies that a prejudicial history has caused, and to eliminate future inequalities.

The current pandemic has graphically exposed the disparities in underlying health conditions between Black and white Americans. Born of the disproportionate economic standards, too many Black Americans have been deprived of health insurance coverage, quality nutrition and consistent access to medical and wellness opportunities.

A national conversation regarding the provision of health insurance, and the likely continuance of varied or transitioning responses to that challenging equation makes projecting a specific program problematic at this time. Fortunately, there are existing opportunities to provide an immediate, if somewhat limited response.

Coinciding with the establishment of the DRE, all Black Americans regardless of age or income should immediately be made eligible for enhanced Medicare coverage (as opposed to Medicaid). By including Part C and D with the standard Medicare, the program will entitle Black Americans to sufficient medical coverage at limited or no cost during the period of transition.

The provision of payment for medical care means considerably less in the absence of convenient access. DRE should establish national programs creating financial incentives and continuing support for expanded health care professionals and facilities in urban, rural and disadvantaged areas that have disproportionate Black

American populations, where persistent racial bias has precluded adequate representation. In addition, the neighborhood facilities envisioned earlier could incorporate certain basic care elements such as providing vaccinations, counseling, prenatal and child care classes and limited elder care.

Quality nutrition is a critical component of a variety of controllable health issues that are prominent in the Black American population, such as obesity, diabetes and hypertension. The general increases in economic stability covered previously should allow for generalized improvements in nutrition quality and quantity, along with the prescribed expansion of SNAP program benefits.

In addition to health care support, opportunities for making better food choices are often denied Black Americans. Predominantly Black or economically challenged communities are often avoided by major grocery chains, restricting selection and raising prices. DRE could establish financial incentive programs for ensuring that all neighborhoods have access to fresh dairy, meats and produce, either through grocery stores or farmer's markets. It could then maintain monitoring programs to ensure that availability and pricing of essential foods remains regionally consistent regardless of location.

In addition to nutrition, access to physical exercise and sports has been curtailed lately due to budgetary constraints, with such reductions specifically impacting Black communities. DRE should evaluate the efficacy of sponsoring or promoting such programs, whether through the indicated school systems or through their own neighborhood facilities.

DRE, through its expansive database, would have a significant opportunity to support and manage critical research into the existing disparities in health and wellness between Black and white Americans. While it is convenient to allocate those differences strictly to economic and environmental challenges, there is an opportunity to combine specific information with policy and program generation that is focused on the results of those findings. DRE -- ideally working with Historic Black Colleges and Universities -- should provide both funding and support for dedicated research towards identifying and addressing any additional or misunderstood issues regarding health factors that are impacting those differentials.

CHAPTER THIRTEEN

Employment

"It's all right to tell a man to lift himself by his own bootstraps, but it is a cruel jest to say to a bootless man that he ought to lift himself by his own bootstraps." Martin Luther King, Jr.

The form of oppression that can be the most debilitating, and in some ways the most cruel, is the denial to a person of the ability to improve their circumstances. Such has been the deliberate and institutionalized reality for Black Americans of virtually every generation in this country.

There are any number of resources and assets that must be provided to Black Americans in the name of reparations, and many of them will be in the form of grants and payments. There is nothing that will be more meaningful to the attainment of racial equality than the full parity of opportunity and the support of individual potential. During his eulogy for George Floyd, the reverend Al Sharpton was passionate:

"... Because ever since 401 years ago, the reason we could never be who we wanted and dreamed to be is you kept your knee on our neck... It is time for us to stand up in George's name and say 'Get your knee off our necks!'"

Amen.

The litany of historic constraints on Black American employment are self-evident and pervasive. Even after the atrocity of slavery ended, no other group of Americans have been the enduring subject of specific governmental limitations, whether on a federal, state or local basis. What is occasionally less obvious are the continuing impact of current constraints and biases in spite of various legislation designed to moderate those disparities.

These persistent discriminatory factors are represented both in terms of related unemployment statistics and in average levels of income and positions held. Black unemployment rates prior to the pandemic were almost double as those for white Americans (1.9x); the majority of the much publicized improvements in those numbers over the past two years (and recently, following the pandemic lows) relate primarily to low wage occupations.

While these stark differences reflect a variety of contributing factors, including racially derived disparities in educational and geographic access, the primary inhibiting factor remains racial bias in hiring and promoting. Studies that introduce candidates of equal quality and interview performance to openings indicate that the resultant hiring statistics fairly accurately mirror the unemployment disparity, supporting racial bias as a meaningful determinant.

It is, unfortunately, not within the power of legislation or governmental authority to remove racial prejudice from the hearts of all white Americans.

What is possible is for the DRE agency to utilize its mandate and unique resources to create, implement and manage programs for the expansion of Black employment in America. This effort should encompass a series of initiatives, including but not limited to the development of incentive based programs for the targeted hiring of Black Americans.

Directed employment of Black Americans through quotas and Affirmative Action programs have previously had mixed results, and have engendered controversy. The DRE efforts can and should be shaped differently, albeit with similar objectives. Rather than dictating mandatory hiring levels in public companies, the DRE initiative would seek to maximize exposure of qualified candidates in conjunction with providing specific financial subsidies related to the hiring of DRE promoted candidates.

Based on a series of parameters, DRE subsidies could range from relief from payroll tax obligations regarding the individual to actual financial compensation for a portion or all of an individual's payroll costs. DRE could tailor the determinations regarding subsidies based on individual qualifications, specified industry, macroeconomic conditions and the related Black employment statistics both in that industry and nationally.

The same metrics for DRE subsidies could be applied to government employment as well as private industry, where the effective transfer of funds could ultimately take different forms and channels. In a particularly dynamic program, DRE would create and support a number of employment opportunities within the dedicated community facilities that it sponsors nationally, where it would systematically encourage internal training and evaluation for promotion within the organization, develop competency for potential entrepreneurial enterprises, and for enhancing those individuals' attractiveness to public companies.

All initiatives would be based on establishing a geographically sensitive database that provided analysis for changing demographic participation and related outcomes by region, industry and on a national basis. Through this analysis, DRE could simultaneously promote Black employment through the proposed and other incentive based programs. It could also use its tools to flag and support the enforcement of existing laws pertaining to racial discrimination.

CHAPTER FOURTEEN

Making It Real

The best intentions are irrelevant without a commitment to, and a solid plan for, effective implementation. We can fill volumes with promises, with the stated aspirations of politicians and leaders who – whether entirely sincere or just pandering – have been featured on the evening news, but the resultant reality always falls well short of the vow.

If reparations are to be comprehensive and enduring, a specific program must emerge that can be enacted and that will have the authority and resources to bring it to fruition. As a businessman, I know just one format for guiding that development: a business plan. Born of that comfort level, this book is intended as a preliminary version of such a plan, one admittedly lacking of the necessary details but one that encourages others to adopt that familiar approach.

In an era of political generalities, there is a distinct lack of actual production on the part of our government. This issue demands more of us. It demands that we adapt the levers of power to the completion of our task, and that we instill in that initiative the true authority for success.

Without such authority, without the substance of institutional presence, there is little in history to recommend trusting in the promises of equality by transient politicians. This time cries out for better than that, and my intention is to provide one guide to that reality.

America has grappled with the concept of reparations since the end of the civil war without any noticeable success. The forces aligned against enacting significant programs for redressing a history of racial abuse and the continuing inequity, or for incurring any major expense on its behalf, have never relented or even been seriously challenged. This is the reality that must be understood, and braced for, in the pursuit of meaningful change.

The struggle to develop a sufficient groundswell of public support, and to make reparations such as are defined herein a reality, requires a massive effort to educate and inform the broad American public. In establishing that necessary agreement and subsequent mandate, it will become apparent that the pursuit of racial equalization is not an event, but a true process that will require dedication and persistence towards a lengthy and in many ways uncertain conclusion.

To engage the country in such a long term project, it is the process itself that must be seen as the immediate contribution to a solution by both Black and white America. That requires a transparent sincerity of intent coupled with an unequivocal authority, one imbued with a healthy dose of self determination by Black society. It must be punctuated with a stated emphasis on both the objectives and quantifiable progress. It will require a central, focused and executable mission, one that articulates both the actual costs and projected outcomes for each initiative.

At the end of the day, the process must incorporate the creation of an authority that is empowered, relatively autonomous and institutionally present at the table of governance. The creation of the DRE will reflect that communal and official commitment, and in so doing, will hopefully deflect to a certain degree the angst regarding the lack of instant gratification. It will provide demonstrable evidence of a change in direction, and a government that has finally listened and can translate what it has heard into action.

While the public will need to see something that it can declare to have been delivered on that promise of change, it is the granular nature of the DRE operations and points of emphasis that will actually transform America. In the case of true racial reparations, it is not the devil that resides in the details, but our better angels.

I am cautioned by the experience of the only similar effort made by the United States that I am aware of; the establishment of the Bureau of Indian Affairs in 1824, and its myriad subsequent iterations. There is little case to be made for the present day results of two centuries of supposed Native American representation; the agency too often became as much a force for punitive measures as for substantive gains during its erratic life, and has been a poster child for financial inefficiency and failure.

In order for the DRE to be accepted as an agent for transformation, the lessons of the BIA must be understood, and differences highlighted. The elevation of the DRE to a full Department (as opposed to the BIA's status as an office within the Department of the Interior) and the possible elevation of the DRE leader to a cabinet level position would be an important demonstration of that separation.

In this regard, there are two additional elements that are critical to both acceptance by an understandably sceptical public, and to its eventual success. First, the operational authority of the DRE must be vested in accepted members of its Black constituency, with an institutional priority of future promotion from within its rank and file. Second, the financial reporting, analysis and projections should be focused on and understood in the totality of their objectives and impacts rather than in their individual components. It is likely, even inevitable, that deficits in one program will be essential to the efficacy of another; it is equally inevitable that early deficits in one program will be offset by later accruals in programs enabled by the loss leader.

The absolute costs of the prescribed programs would be best expressed publicly through a formulaic prism, where specific expenses are contrasted to the broader benefits accrued, as demonstrated in the following examples:

- The economic impact nationally from the resultant increase in disposable income and increased home ownership
- The increase in local, state and federal tax revenues generated by elevated wage earnings and expanded property ownership
- The value to the national GDP of the increased national productivity
- The cost savings from decreased levels of incarceration and subsequent management
- The economic impact and employment effect of increased entrepreneurial activity
- The cost savings from decreased levels of dependency on governmental aid and other social programs
- The economic impact of a diminished consumption of uninsured health and

wellness resources in what has been a disproportionately indigent population

There are any number of additional benefits relating to an improved stability of families and communities, and the resultant reduction of racial strife. The establishment of the DRE may be complex to envision, but can be simplified through emphasis on its structural organization, operational logistics and its concentration on effective channels of distribution.

In establishing a new Department that was charged with promoting racial equality in America, much of the energy towards reparations would have a focal point and reason for advocacy and policy contributions. The origination of DRE would incorporate divisions relating to economic equality, housing fairness, business development, social justice, voter rights, political representation and data collection and management.

DRE's mission must be direct, something along the following lines:

The DRE is created for the establishment and management of government programs to redress existing

inequalities born of racial injustice and systemic discrimination in America.

Specifically, DRE will provide for the rectification of historic and enduring deprivations of opportunities and equality in the areas of economic, educational, environmental, vocational, representational and social justice due to racism in American laws, policies and society.

DRE will further institute such programs and policies as will insure and protect racial equality in all present and future American policies and practices.

The initiation of DRE's authority would include a range of programs based on three key resources:

1. The creation, execution and management of a national network of community based facilities that would have the capacity and authority to implement and support both DRE programming and aligned Social Services.

2. The creation and submission of such laws, programs, governance, allocations and guidance as are deemed appropriate by the

DRE for achieving the objectives of its mission.

3. The application, allocation and distribution of such funds as are requested by the DRE and Congressionally approved for use under its auspices and mandates.

In the period of its inception, DRE would have a number of critical initiatives within its authority. Those would encompass the following areas:

- Poverty Remediation
- Economic Opportunity
- Educational Advancement
- Promotion of Historical Accuracies
- Housing Equality
- Business Development
- Social Justice
- Voting Rights Protection and Representation
- Public Policy Advocacy
- Data and Information Acquisition and Management

If the initiatives are prepared and approved by the time the DRE is approved, then the programs in response to these areas could be enacted in conjunction with the agency; if they are not, then the DRE should be empowered when ready. The timeliness of this installation and the role that it might play in advancing its causes cannot be overstated, and should not be compromised by the desire for completion. Following its initiation and the appointment of the Department head, the resulting division hierarchy and technical support would be best able to create the information and public pressure needed to usher the necessary legislation through Congress from official positions.

The halls of government are littered with the sacrificial carcasses of good programs that were abandoned once they became postponed and delayed. The creation, funding and installation of the DRE would cement the functional start of a critical journey to redemption and fairness, allowing the best possible foundation for future successes.

CHAPTER FIFTEEN

A Present and Unprecedented Opportunity

History is often a collection of confluences. It has seen the matching of men and women with circumstances and events; it has provided natural occurrences that aligned with human development. History has a way of matchmaking, usually in ways that we could never have predicted, or planned.

In this moment in time, America is finally awake to and aware of the depths of our racial inequality in ways that have (inconceivably) escaped its notice for centuries. A collapsed economy, a politically rife moment in time, a pandemic that has paralyzed the nation may seem at first glance a strange stimulus for positive social consciousness, but it is not really… transformation almost always occurs against the backdrop of calamity and chaos.

It is in this moment that we find everything aligned, from financial reordering to governmental transition, from public support to catalyzing events. If we grasp the opportunity with both hands, if we take this moment and freeze it in our sights, there is an unprecedented opportunity for that transformational change. We must not lose this moment. This momentum and structural opportunity may not come again, and if it does, we may not be up to the challenge.

We are, we must be, up to it now.

The resources required -- in dollars, time and congressional energy and will -- to establish the organization, the programs and the indicated infrastructure for reparations will be, by any possible measure, substantial. The final numbers will be daunting, and their sheer size will be noted as sufficient reason for not engaging in the process by far too many in and out of government. Before the year 2020, that argument might have had some teeth... After all, no government can be expected to make a commitment that goes beyond its capacity to pay, can it?

Perhaps not… but in the words of our financial and monetary leadership, that's really not a problem, at least not in this time and place. Here is some context, and an explanation.

In response to the financial aspects of the pandemic-related financial crisis of 2020, Congress, the Treasury Department and the Federal Reserve have allocated literally trillions of dollars, derived both from future tax revenues and some hyperactive printing presses, to stem the worst of the challenges. Those trillions have been made available at nominal or zero interest rates, and hundreds of billions have been provided to multinational organizations through a number of hastily formulated channels.

The acceptance of the resulting deficits, unprecedented and previously unimaginable, provide a surprising opportunity for envisioning the necessary funding to address racial inequality appropriately. The creation of numerous credit facilities by the Federal Reserve, and the development of new channels of distribution by the Treasury have created an infrastructure that can accommodate massive amounts of capital flow; the artificial compression of interest rates to historically low levels has created a political acceptance of the extreme national debt structure, and an understanding that comprehensive and long term efforts will be required to address it.

Into that environment comes a specific and timely logic, an argument that is unique to the moment.

As could hardly be surprising, the most painful tolls of the twin calamities of health issues and economic distress fell disproportionately on the heads of Black (and brown) Americans. The historic issues that have led to an absence of developed financial reserves, the health issues that have evolved from generational poverty and lack of resources, and the employment issues that found Black workers populating the most vulnerable positions in commerce have proven to be a perfect storm.

Hospitalizations from Covid-19 the and resultant deaths, the unemployment and sudden poverty have all impacted minority communities far more severely than they have white communities. Ironically the same afflicted minority populations man the most essential services and incur the greatest risks on behalf of the rest of America. Even without the necessary conversations about reparations, the gross inequality exposed by the virus and economic collapse would argue loudly for the need of a dedicated response.

In the context of the larger obligations, that urgent attention is inextricably intertwined with what is already owed to Black Americans. It is merely the latest entry in a centuries old ledger, another bit of red ink in a vast sea of it.

The collision of traumatic economic damage with the broadly accepted need to address racial inequality and historic predation provides both the impetus and opportunity for constructive urgency. Unique in the past 150 years, this confluence of societal awareness, structural capability and the need for a national reset of economic policy provides a critical opening.

Those trillions of dollars provided will manifest themselves as part of the national debt, elevating that total to levels never before assumed as possible. When asked about the future of the necessary payments, the Secretary of the Treasury responded flippantly: "Interest rates are incredibly low, so there is very little cost of borrowing this money," Stephen Mnuchin told reporters. "And as I've said, in different times we'll fix the deficit. This is not the time to worry about it." Later on, Mnuchin would float the idea of creating ultra long term Treasury instruments, bonds with maturities of 50 or 100 years, in order to restructure existing debt and to take advantage of artificially lowered rates.

Simultaneously, comments from Federal Reserve Chairman Jerome Powell sounded an equally optimistic note, at least in regards to the funding of the Dow. Faced with an extraordinary challenge, Powell confirmed that he had access to "unlimited amounts of funds" to buttress the economy, a brash statement that he supported by announcing a series of credit facilities designed to act as conduits for trillions of dollars of credit without interest costs.

The Treasury and the Fed have now publicly illustrated the unconstrained capacity of both Fiscal and Monetary programs to respond creatively to special needs. In the present times, those capacities are significantly expanded by historically low rates on borrowing, with interest rates being held at or close to zero intentionally as a means for supporting the economic recovery. All in all, it leads to a powerful conclusion:

There has never been, and will likely never be again, a superior moment to effect the structural changes and incur the expenses of the reparation programs outlined here:

- Federal interest rates are at historic lows, providing minimized costs for long term borrowing. Within the existing additions to the long term debt, and the required policies for adapting to an unprecedented servicing requirement, the supplemental amounts required for addressing racial inequality would have a controllable impact on the credit markets.

- Programs for broad economic development are being formulated, and will likely be a priority for several years. Paramount will be a recreation of the nation's unemployment facilities, exposed as inadequate and antiquated by the financial crisis. Incorporating -- and more importantly, implementing -- the programs described earlier will be enabled as a byproduct of those necessary renovations.

- Unprecedented credit facilities are already in place, supporting the logistics for the distribution of large amounts of capital across potentially millions of recipients. The financial support for Black owned businesses, both small and large, could be supported by the existing fiscal and monetary infrastructure without substantial alteration.

- Construction and infrastructure programs that are national in scope are specifically needed and equally attractive to both parties, a rare point of policy agreement. The distributed nature of the indicated community centers is a perfect fit, and the type of project that can be rapidly initiated. Similarly, expanded demand for housing based on the reduced costs for Black Americans would fit effectively inside of that same equation.

- The Affordable Care Act, under aggressive attack since its difficult inception, will be substantially revised and possibly replaced by whichever party ascends in the 2020 elections, coming just as millions of Americans have lost their coverage along with their jobs. The resulting legislation will open opportunities for the incorporation of remedial programs for Black Americans.

- Needed adjustments to policies and programs regarding excessive incarceration have a discernible financial benefit, a rare opportunity to incorporate structural improvements with significant cost savings. Coupled with the growing national movement towards legalization or decriminalization for lower level drug offenses, a re-envisioning of sentencing guidelines, work programs and a massive release for existing non-violent offenders should align with existing political momentum.

- Expansive policy proposals by the Democratic party regarding child care and pre-k schooling will almost assuredly become legislative discussions after the 2020 election, offering a perfect point of entry for the programs described herein. In addition, the impact of the pandemic on school structures and budgets at all levels suggest a significant reappraisal of funding levels and federal support for student debt, creating in turn access points for instituting the grant programs suggested herein.

Hard as it is to reconcile the almost existential pain of these times with a term such as opportunity, it fits here. Virtually every aspect of the necessary economic recovery coincides with one or more aspects of the programs and policies of effective reparations. Every circumstance of the present fiscal and monetary policy promotes introduction of the specific financial requirements. Dynamic changes in legislative priorities relate directly to the overflowing energies of a generational public movement.

There is no good in the deaths of so many, or in the suffering that has ensued and spread across the country and the world. In our inefficiency and division, we have missed countless opportunities to moderate the pain, and continue to do so. There is no joy in the events that have led to so many marching. The strife and unrest of an afflicted nation has its roots in exposed evil, not uncovered treasures.

That is all without debate.

It is also without reasonable debate that the necessary changes on behalf of racial injustice and inequity, so long delayed and denied, have their moment in the present, and that the circumstances of their arrival are perfectly aligned.

It is critical that we not miss those signs, and that we see this chance through while we have it in our grasp.

CHAPTER SIXTEEN

The Case for Why This, Why Now

The acceptance of responsibility by white America for historical and contemporary racism in our laws, our institutions and our society is irrefutable and urgent. The decision to respond to those transgressions and to resolve their impact on Black Americans is a moral imperative, one that we cannot continue to avoid or diminish. It is an essential medicine for an ailing nation, a prescription for an illness that has lingered for centuries, corroding our national soul. It is right and just.

It is not just some abstract punishment. The recalibration of American society towards equality and fairness is not merely the necessary and right thing for us to do; it is also a critical component to a better America, a country that can finally manifest its true destiny. In relieving the yoke of racial oppression, our nation will have for the first time a commonality in rowing towards our best future, with all arms unchained and lifting up the weights of our coming challenges.

In true reparations, there are three distinct commitments that must be engaged as they affect white America:

1. *To openly acknowledge and address the pervasive transgression of endemic racism*

2. *To actively respond to the present conditions and circumstances of the victims of our oppression*

3. *To support the necessary and appropriate steps to realize a nation consistent with our stated principals, one that enjoys the benefits of the full potential of all of its citizens.*

The complications of the present world are unprecedented in our lifetimes, and demonstrably expanding. The future is not a given, and even before the complicating arrival of the Coronavirus, the present was compromised. We have been beset by the incomplete transition to integrated global economies, and to militarized politics across a rapidly shifting global alignment. Economic frailty, exposed and exacerbated by the pandemic, threatens the assumed prosperity of most of the world and potentially the stability of even the most powerful nations. Environmental challenges suggest an expanding frequency and growing impact of random crises, and a critical need for international cooperation in dealing with their causes and effects.

Success in responding to these massive and predictable challenges requires that America, for decades the indisputable global leader, assert that preeminence from a position of maximal strength and internal efficiency. We will be called on to either return to that chair at the head of the table, or to make room for ascendant powers that are not our allies to replace us. Into this fraught and dynamic environment, America presents itself today at its weakest and most unworthy of dominance. This must be rectified, and without delay, for the good of not only this nation, but of the world.

The primary elements of an American resurgence must begin with a cooling down of the inflammatory divisions roiling our country. For America to effectively lead, it must heal itself and in so doing, offer the world a prescription for doing the same in their own lands. The path to resolution of the present political schism is unclear, except that beginning that work depends on our administration's approach changing from intentional instigation to deliberate de-escalation, a seemingly impossible conversion without a drastic change through the 2020 elections.

The other dominant internal conflict should logically not be a conflict at all. Racism -- historic, systemic or present -- is indefensible and specifically contrary to our stated national value system. There should be a universal mandate for the condemnation and elimination of racial inequality in every aspect of American life. It should transcend party lines and generational preferences.

And yet… racism in all of its forms persists, and the present conversation about it is still elementary, no more than a shaky start. That discussion needs to escalate immediately and quickly into meaningful recognition and commitment to action. If there is some residual reluctance, the conversation should be put into a simple context:

The challenges before America are momentous. Our future will be determined by our present. We need the full and unconflicted participation of a complete country to address them, yet fully an eighth of the country continues to be constrained by the centuries old shackles of imposed predation. Becoming more aware now, America is embroiled by its residual and present national guilt, and its global leadership is compromised by its apparent inability or willingness to respond.

America must release its Black citizens from the constrictions it has imposed on them, recalibrate their evolved deficits, and empower them to participate and contribute to a national rebirth. There are no real choices (as if there ever should have been) and no more time for denial or delay.

The history of racial oppression and pervasive abuse is a dominant aspect in the development of virtually every aspect of America. It is a demonstrable defect in the national DNA, and it has infected every generation since the founding of this nation. The resultant inequality remains today, both as a visible product of generational deprivations and in the persistent reality of present bias. The damages inflicted on Black Americans by systemic racism are essentially incalculable, and its continuation incessantly adds to that deficit.

In the present moment, a mass exposure of the murder of Black Americans by police officers has forced a revelatory conversation about racial inequality. Prompted by public support of, and participation in, national and international protests and condemnation, a coalition of political, cultural and economic forces have cracked open a door to meaningful discussions.

For America to accept responsibility for its exploitation of a significant portion of its own citizens, the resulting conversation must provide for three primary outcomes: a redressing of prior deprivations, a recalibration of the present condition, and the establishment of a constructive foundation for future equality.

The effective resolution of those objectives requires a comprehensive matrix of legislative policies and programs, substantially committing the nation's efforts and resources to the task. The benefits of doing so are not only the restoration of our national moral standing, but are tangibly vital to America's best future.

In order to address any of the critical issues of racial inequality, it is necessary to address all of them. Solutions for poverty are irrelevant if employment and business opportunities are not improved. The solutions for housing are potentially temporary if they are not accompanied by representation to protect and preserve those practices. Reforming a predatory system of incarceration is hollow without a concurrent addressing enforcement and judicial standards and practices. Cash payments of any amount, of any kind, in the name of reparations are simply an inefficient process of deferring necessary change, and a cheap salving of a greater guilt.

Given the pervasive nature of American injustice in racial affairs, the list of areas that require substantial change is long and condemning. At its core, any relevant response to transgressions past and present would need to include essentially all of the following:

- Substantial improvements in educational infrastructure, opportunity and available resources
- A reconciliation of historic housing inequity, and its impact on present circumstances
- Remedial opportunities for business development and financing
- A reconfiguration of the composition of law enforcement organization and standards for incarceration

- The acknowledgement of governmental responsibility for, and the active redressing of, generational poverty
- A critical intervention in racially delineated disparities in health, health insurance and wellbeing
- A proactive engagement toward escalating Black employment opportunity and advancement
- An aggressive protection of enduring voter rights and political representation

Presented with an unprecedented ability to self create and to exercise the freedoms of its inception, America has all too often misused that opportunity. It has systematically mistaken power for goodness, and economic success for earned authority, only to be somewhat reigned back to a better path by the inspired blessing of its democracy.

The result -- a nation of unmatched gifts and wealth -- stands not as a monument to persistent righteousness, but rather a complicated outcome of its rampant strength expressed through a line of actions both good and evil. America has done wonderful things, standing as a leader in saving the world from fascism and sharing the innovative fruits of its dynamic economic system. It has, in many lights and many ways, historically been a sanctuary for those seeking nothing greater than the freedoms promised to any who find their way to its shores.

It is tragically ironic that its greatest transgression, its most blatant evil born of greed and misunderstood power, comes from the abject denial of those very freedoms on an inhuman level to an entire race of Americans. The country's grudging progress in overcoming its sin of oppression is, and always has been, insufficient. In this moment of belated enlightenment, there is a possible path to reparation, a process by which some portion of the pervasive oppression of one in eight of our American citizens can begin to be repudiated and healed.

The path before us can be mapped and marked, and we can proceed apace. It is a matter of finding a national will to do so, and a full understanding of the better nation that awaits at the end of that journey. It is the time to take those steps forward.

CHAPTER SEVENTEEN

Epilogue

If we were offered the apple unbit, the tree full of fruit and the serpent unbidden, would we choose to eat from it again?

Original sin is rarely revisited, and in this case, it still might not truly be. The victims of slavery, the generations of Black Americans that have passed without redress, cannot now be given peace. That noted, we are faced with this simple, undeniable point: we have before us a choice. We can either recommit to racial inequality and oppressive prejudice, or we can actively select and empower an alternative future, one of fairness and equality.

What we no longer have is the ability to pretend that it is not our choice.

The original sin of America cannot be redeemed; the generations of the innocent victims of that offense are beyond our capacity to comfort. It is in the expanded awareness of the depth of those transgressions, for too long hidden by shame, greed and prejudice, that the opportunity for the committing of an entirely new sin is being placed squarely in front of white America.

We now understand. We now have the capacity to respond. For us to deny this opportunity, to turn from that obligation and to cling to our ill-gotten privileges and wealth as some twisted substitute for the morality that we profess to be guided by, would be a wholly new transgression against our common humanity.

Jesus Christ once said "...because thou hast seen me, thou hast believed: blessed [are] they that have not seen, and [yet] have believed." (John 20:29)

If we choose to absolve ourselves of our previous blindness to the realities of racial inequality, to declare that our unseeing was simply the result of a system that saw no benefit in exposing it, then that is shameful but irrelevant to the matter at hand. Too much of America has touched the wound where the spear pierced flesh; too many have had their eyes opened now, and see.

To fail to act in concert towards meaningful and sincere reparations and a concordant healing of our American soul is to accept that we, as a nation and as a divided people, are determined to be irredeemable. It is to be presented with the indisputable choice between good and evil, and to have turned in the wrong direction. For the sake of America, the turn to good must come here and now. It must be without hesitation or limitation, but with an open and repentant heart, and a sincere wishing for the elevation of and sharing with all of our citizens.

We cannot change the past, but we must take the difficult steps necessary to dilute the impact of its ravages on the present, and to actively remove it from our future.

The Insufficiency of Reparations is intended as a personal contribution to a critically important national conversation. The ultimate solutions will be informed by the input of many thousands of perspectives and understandings, a coming together of the diverse and exceptional thoughts of all of America.

If you'd like to share your own thoughts and ideas on specific and structural ways that we can use to address racial inequality in America, or if you'd simply like to respond and comment on the ways that I've suggested, please go to: www.theinsufficiencyofreparations.com

To reach out to me personally, please email me at: gary@theinsufficiencyofreparations.com